Touring the LAKE DISTRICT

Jim Watson

High Yewdale Farm, Coniston

CITY BOOKS • BATH • ENGLAND

Watendlath

First published 2021 All rights reserved.

No part of this publication may be reproduced, stored in a retrieval system or recorded by any means, without prior written permission from the author

Text, illustrations and maps © Jim Watson 2021

City Books, c/o
Survival Books Limited,
Office 169, 3 Edgar Buildings,
George Street, Bath BA1 2FJ, United Kingdom
Tel: +44 (0)01225-422884 email: info@survivalbooks.net
websites: citybooks.co/survivalbooks.net
londonssecrets.com

British Library Cataloguing in Publication Data
A CIP record for this book is available
from the British Library.
ISBN: 978-1-913171-22-3

Printed via D'Print Pte Ltd (Singapore)

Cover: Autumn Mist at Thirlspot

Contents

NORTH WEST

1. **DERWENT WATER & BUTTERMERE ROUND**   6
   Keswick – Derwent Water – Rosthwaite – Seatoller – Honister Pass – Buttermere – Newlands Hause – Stair – Grange – Keswick. 26 miles

2. **BRAITHWAITE, NEWLANDS & WHINLATTER ROUND**   24
   Braithwaite – Newlands – Buttermere – Crummock Water – Loweswater – Lorton – Whinlatter Pass – Braithwaite. 24 miles

3. **GRASMERE TO BASSENTHWAITE**   36
   Grasmere – Dunmail Raise – Thirlmere – Keswick bypass – Braithwaite – Bassenthwaite Lake – Bassenthwaite village. 25 miles

4. **THE LANGDALES**   50
   Grasmere – Elterwater – Chapel Style – Great Langdale – Dungeon Ghyll – Blea Tarn – Little Langdale – Skelwith Bridge – Ambleside. 15 miles

Ullswater fells from Pooley Bridge

NORTH EAST

5. **RHEGED to AMBLESIDE**   64
   Rheged – Dalemain – Pooley Bridge – Ullswater – Aira Force – Glenridding – Patterdale – Hartsop – Brotherswater – Kirkstone Pass – Troutbeck – Ambleside. 30 miles

6. **KESWICK, BACK O' SKIDDAW & CALDBECK ROUND**   80
   Keswick – Uldale – Back o' Skiddaw – Caldbeck – Hesket Newmarket – Mungrisdale – Threlkeld – Keswick. 33 miles

SOUTH WEST

7. **LAKELAND DRAMA**   92
   Ambleside – Little Langdale – Wrynose Pass – Cockley Beck – Hardknott Pass – Boot – Eskdale Green – Santon Bridge – Wastwater – Wasdale Head – Gosforth. 36 miles

8. **LAKELAND ICONS**   106
   Brockhole – Windermere – Orrest Head – Bowness – Windermere Ferry – Sawrey – Hawkshead – Tarn Hows – Brantwood – Coniston – Skelwith Bridge – Ambleside – Rydal – Grasmere. 30 miles

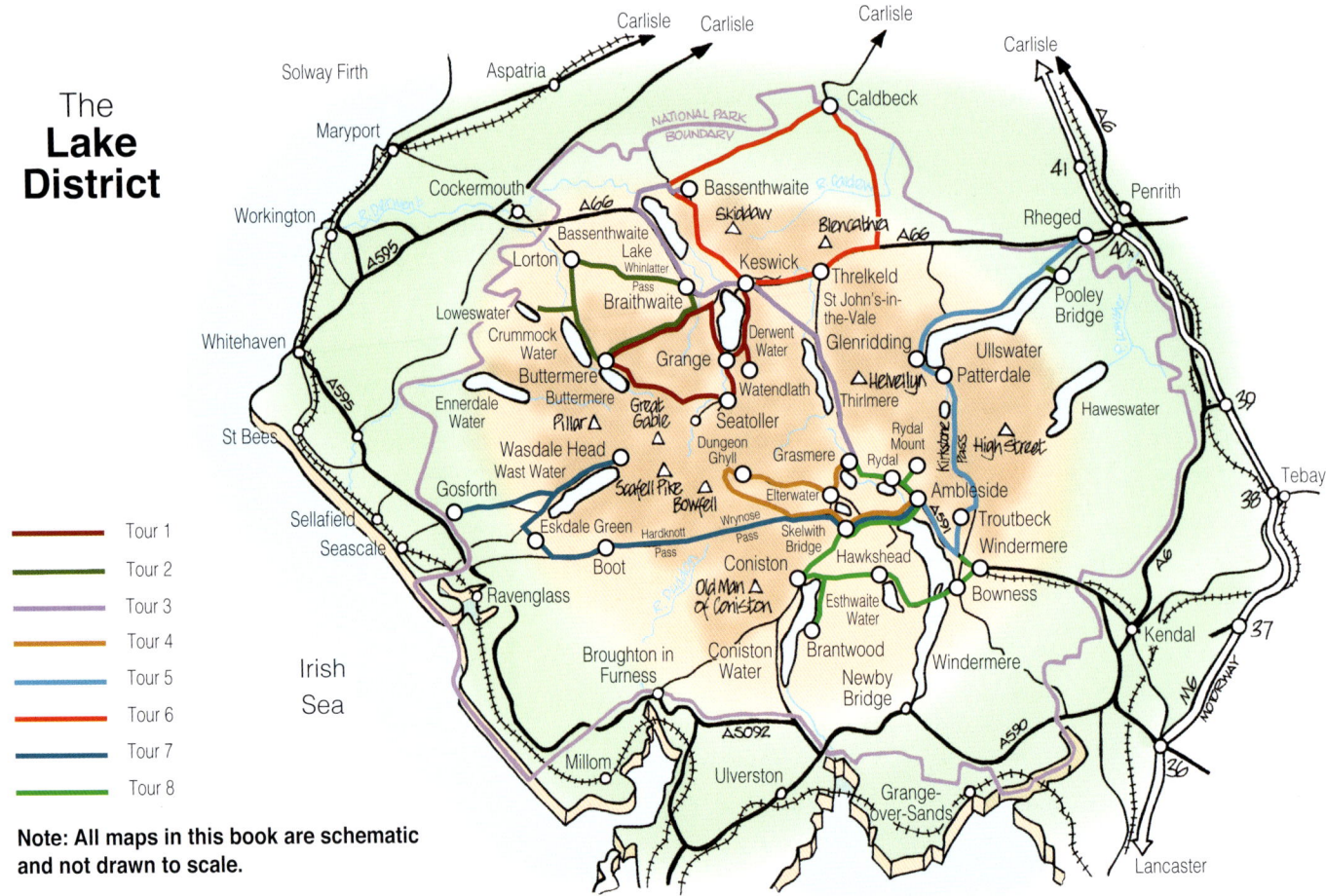

Introduction

Though the largest of the English National Parks, the Lake District is only about 30 miles across and 40 miles from north to south, similar in size to Greater London. Traffic on the M6 motorway speeds past in not much more than half an hour, some drivers never knowing what they're missing.

The mountains are high compared with others in England and the lakes are large in British terms, but on the world stage they're mere molehills and ponds. It's the variety and concentration of good things packed into such a small area that makes the Lake District so special. You don't have to travel far to be thrilled by something.

This book contains eight tours around some of the area's most loved and dramatic locations. They'll take you on the main tourist trails but also to quieter, less-commercialised parts, where life moves at a slower pace and you can savour expansive views of the magnificent mountains and rolling countryside.

The Lake District is also foodie heaven these days, attracting top awards, often for restaurants or pubs in out of the way places, many of which are included in the tours. Lakeland farms have also become excellent pitstops where you can have a break to enjoy home-cooked cakes, scones or pies with your coffee.

The routes range between 15 and 36 miles which allows time for visiting attractions, strolling round villages or just enjoying the blissful views.

Bear in mind that traffic on the main roads can be heavy, particularly at weekends. Tour 7 crosses Wrynose and Hardknott passes, described as the 'most spectacular and steepest' roads in Britain. Though an exhilarating and dramatic test of driving skills they are not for the fainthearted, and shouldn't be undertaken in bad weather.

Take care and happy motoring!

Jim Watsero

Rugby, 2021

Please note ...

Much of this book was prepared during the Covid pandemic outbreak of 2019, when opening times or closures of many attractions and pitstops were unpredicable. Always check ahead before setting out on a tour.

An old oven in a wall at Hartsop (Possibly to keep milk deliveries cool)

TOUR 1

Derwent Water & Buttermere Round • 26 miles

Keswick – Derwent Water – Rosthwaite – Seatoller – Honister Pass – Buttermere – Newlands Hause – Stair – Grange – Keswick

Add 5 miles if you visit Watendlath

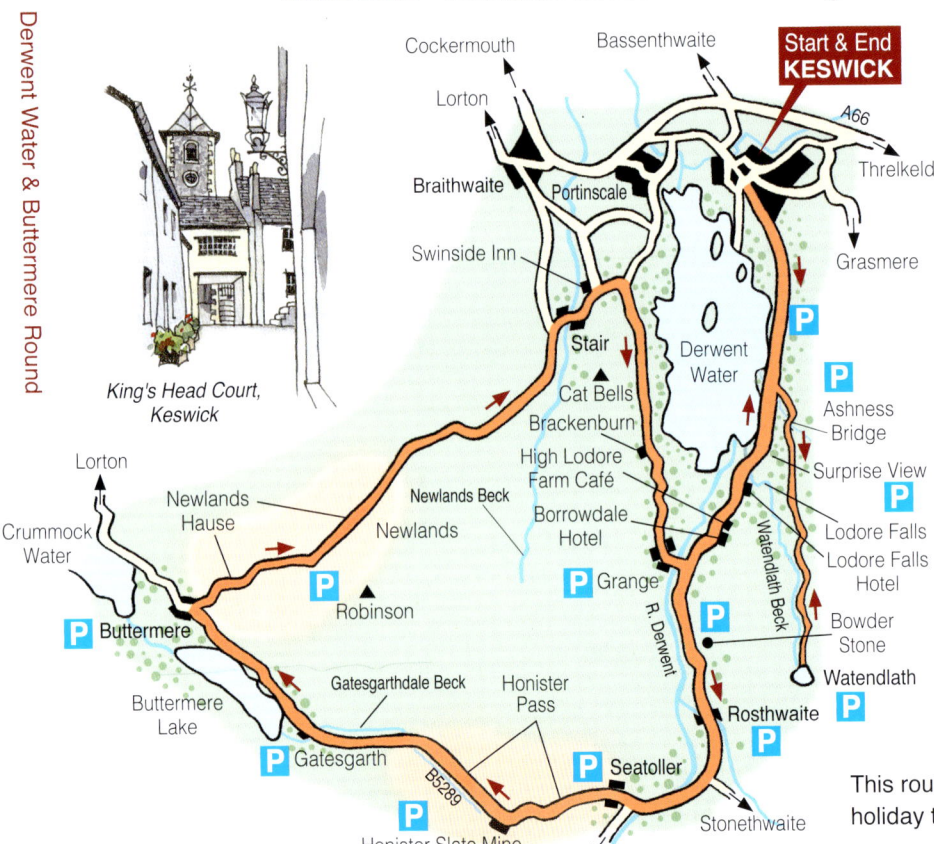

This tour begins on the the B5289 out of Keswick, one of the Lake District's most scenic roads, travelling south through most of Borrowdale. The road follows the eastern shore of Derwent Water, generally regarded as 'the Queen of the Lakes'.

A detour climbs to a tranquil 'hanging valley' with idyllic Watendlath at its head. The narrow access road twists along wooded clifftops with many famous views along the way.

Beyond the head of Derwent Water the valley narrows dramatically through the 'Jaws of Borrowdale'. From Seatoller you climb Honister Pass into Buttermere, less pretty than Borrowdale but more rugged and spectacular. After turning east to cross Newlands Hause you descend gently down the alluring Newlands valley.

Finally the route turns south across the lower slopes of Cat Bells for unbeatable views across Derwent Water, before rejoining the B5289 back to Keswick.

This route is very popular and often busy, especially at holiday times. The only petrol stations are in Keswick.

Keswick

This old market town of tightly packed slate buildings is fabulously set between Derwent Water and Skiddaw, with Borrowdale and the high mountains stretching away to the south.

Keswick developed along with the 18th-century mining industry and the world's first pencils were made here using graphite mined in Borrowdale. With the relocation of the pencil mill to Workington in 2008, Keswick is now totally given over to tourism.

Despite its dedication to outdoor activites and the huge range of equipment you apparently need to enjoy them, Keswick has 'proper' shops and some decent art galleries. There's also a market held on the open area around the Moot Hall every Thursday and Saturday with a wide range of local products and food on sale, including Artisan cheeses, Herdwick sheep fleeces and designer wooley jumpers.

The River Greta winds attractively around the town, peaceably enough generally but after heavy rain it swells to a raging torrent, bringing devastating flooding and damage to many parts. Storm Desmond in December 2015 was particularly destructive.

Originally built in 1571 and rebuilt in 1695, the present Moot Hall dates to 1813. It's seen service as a courthouse, prison, market, museum and town hall. An unusual one-handed clock in the tower used to be wound every day by a diligent local man. Since 1971, the ground floor has been used as a National Park Information Bureau, the busiest in Lakeland.

Keswick Main Street & the Moot Hall

1

Derwent Water & Buttermere Round

Pencil Museum Located on the site of the original factory, the museum reopened in 2017 after disastrous flood damage in the 2015 storm. It tells you all you need to know about pencils, including history, and demonstrations. The world's largest colour pencil is on show. It's almost 26ft long. And yellow.

Fitz Park Play area, games' courts for football and basketball. BMX track. Upper Fitz Park is a more formal area with landscaped gardens and an arboretum. Also has a 18-hole putting green, bowls and croquet.

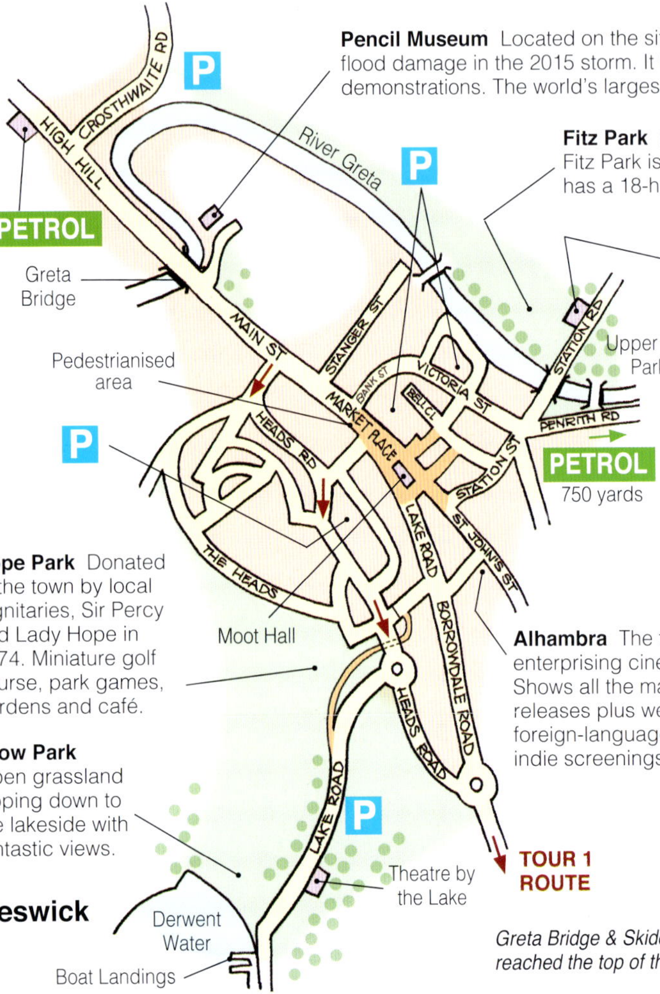

Museum & Art Gallery
Founded in 1873 with the Fitz Park building opening in 1898 and the Art Gallery added in 1905. A major renovation in 2014 added an extension and the Café West. Its varied collections feature the area's landscape, history and culture, including manuscripts of all the Lakeland poets and numerous 'oddities'.

The most famous exhibit is the Musical Stones collected on Skiddaw by stone mason, Joseph Richardson in the 1830s, which sound in tune when struck. Toured Victorian England as the 'Rock, Bell and Steel Band'.

Museum & Art Gallery

Hope Park Donated to the town by local dignitaries, Sir Percy and Lady Hope in 1974. Miniature golf course, park games, gardens and café.

Crow Park Open grassland sloping down to the lakeside with fantastic views.

Alhambra The town's enterprising cinema. Shows all the mainstream releases plus weekly foreign-language and indie screenings.

Keswick

TOUR 1 ROUTE

Greta Bridge & Skiddaw. Flood water reached the top of the bridge walls in 2015

8

Castlerigg Stone Circle

Set on a hilltop 1.5 miles east of Keswick town centre is the finest Neolithic circle in the Lakes.

Castlerigg consists of thirty-nine stones arranged in an oval whose greatest diameter is 110ft. Contained within it is a unique rectangle of stones. The tallest stands just over seven feet, average height is three feet. They are reckoned to be between 3 to 4,000 years old; ancient when the Romans were here. Why the stones were erected at this spot and what their purpose was is an enduring mystery.

There are seventeen other Neolithic circles in the Lake District, some even more impressive then Castlerigg. But none enjoy the marvellous setting that this one has, perched on its grassy eminence 650ft above the streets of Keswick and surrounded by some of Lakeland's finest fells. Breathtaking with snow on the tops or during a sunset over Skiddaw.

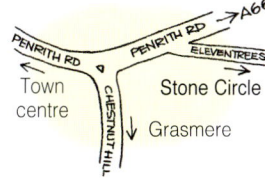

Castlerigg Stone Circle & Blencathra

PIT STOPS

The town enjoys a rich *smorgasbord* of eating and drinking establishments. This is only a tiny selection:

Morrel's, Lake Road
Keswick's top eating spot serving Modern British and Mediterranean styles. Closest restaurant to the Theatre by the Lake. *morrels.co.uk*

Inn on the Square, Market Square
Caters for all tastes. Award-winning Brossen Steakhouse for night time dining. The uber modern Front Bar serves brunch, lunches and home-made cakes. The dog-loving and family friendly Back Bar overlooks the Bell Close car park. *innonthesquare.co.uk*

Dog & Gun, Lake Road
Tradition pub with oak beams and stone floors. Pub grub *par excellence* with gourmet chips. Popular with locals as well as visitors. Gets crowded. *greeneking-pubs.co.uk*

Abraham's Café, Lake Road
Praised for its soups, big breakfasts and open sandwiches. Located on the top floor of Fisher's famous store, there are a lot stairs to ascend. Well, it is a climbing shop, after all – and the views are great. *georgefisher.co.uk/cafe*

Wetherspoon, Bank Street.
The brand's excellent value for money food and ale. Located in the former magistrates' court and police station, rejoicing in the glorious name of The Chief Justice of the Common Pleas. *jdwetherspoon.com*

Keswick also boasts some excellent **fish & chip shops**. The Kingfisher in Main Street and The Lakes Fish & Chips in Bank Street are recommended.

1

Derwent Water & Buttermere Round

With upmarket gift shops, restaurants, cafés, bistros, bars and pubs, Lake Road is Keswick's most hip & happening street.

Look out for the 12ft-tall metal giraffe outside the Treeby & Bolton store. It was made of recycled oil drums by a team of ten artists in Kenya and shipped here in a giant container. Apart from the popular sculpture, Treeby & Bolton also boasts a fashionable shop, gallery and café.

George Fisher opened in 1957, when it was the first to import mountain equipment from Austria. Since then it has become one of the most celebrated outdoors store in the Lakes.

A quiet day in Lake Road

Hailed 'the most beautifully located and friendly theatre in Britain', the Theatre by the Lake was opened in 1999, replacing the unlovely mobile Century Theatre. With a full programme of drama, concerts, exhibitions and events, it has established Keswick as the main cultural centre for the northern Lake District. A coffee shop and bar are open on performance days.

Theatre by the Lake

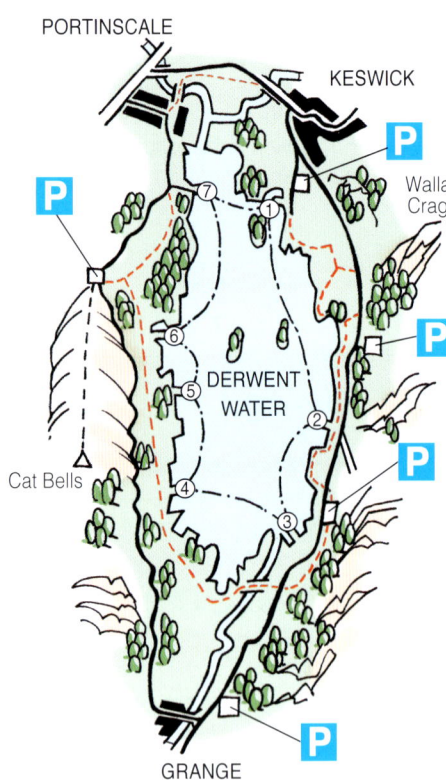

Derwent Water has long been regarded as one of the most attractive of all the lakes. Add Borrowdale and in this valley, more perfectly than anywhere else in the Lake District, are found the three components of the Romantic Ideal – rock, trees and water – in glorious abundance. A splendid walk of about 10 miles goes all round the lake, with only the short stretch between Nickol End and Keswick being away from the lakeside.

Launch landing stages
1. Keswick 2. Ashness Gate
3. Lodore 4. High Brundlehow
5. Low Brundelhow 6. Hawse End
7. Nichol End

Derwent Water

Widest of all the lakes, Derwentwater is around three miles long and just over one mile wide with a maximum depth of 72ft. There are four main islands plus nine smaller ones.

A visit to Keswick is incomplete without a walk down to the lake. It's less than a mile from central Keswick and the view from the boat landings is one of the most admired in Lakeland.

The Keswick launches have run a regular service calling at seven landing stages around the lake since 1904. Two of the boats still in use were built of Burma teak over 80 years ago, originally for the exclusive use of Lodore Hotel residents.

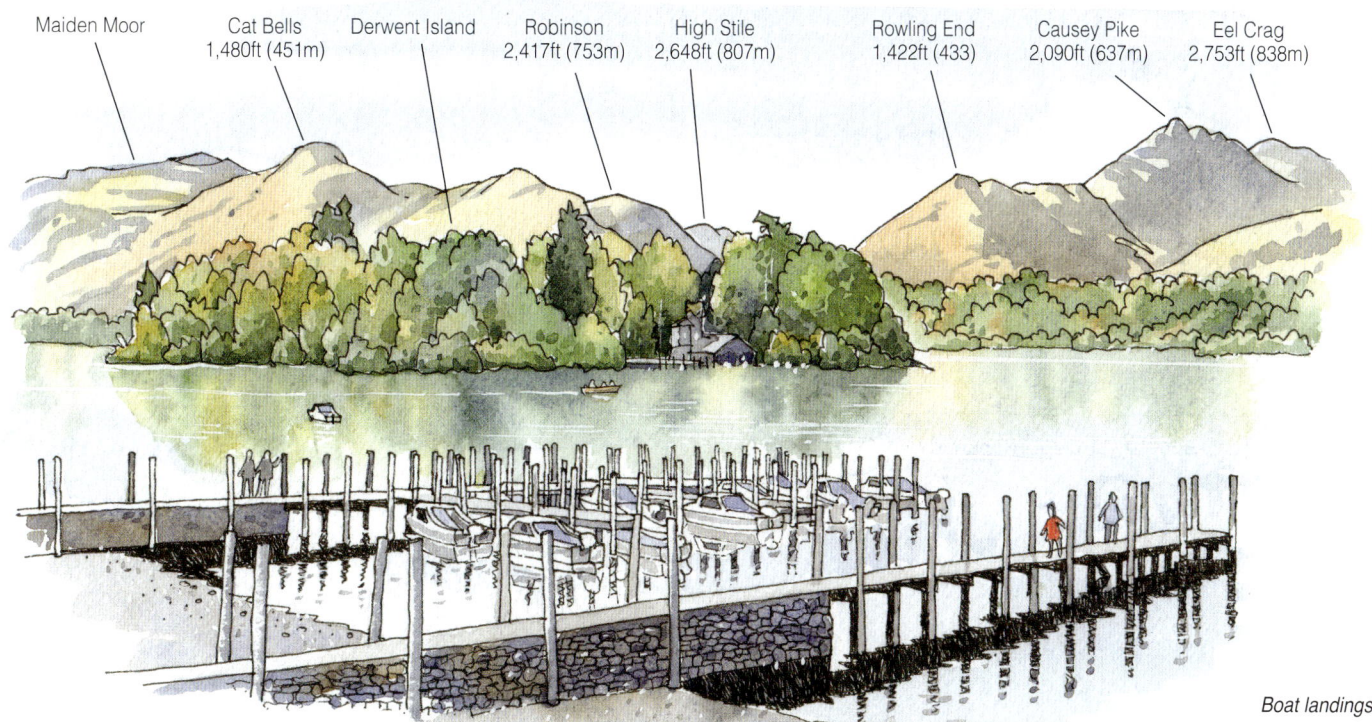

Boat landings

1

Derwent Water & Buttermere Round

Friar's Crag is one of the most visited spots in Lakeland. It's only a low headland of rock topped by scraggy Scots pines and hardly rates the 'crag' tag. However, as a vantage point it is beyond compare. The art critic and social thinker, John Ruskin, who has a memorial on the crag, rated the view of Borrowdale from Friar's Crag in his top three in Europe, though he was prone to hyperbole. According to him Keswick was 'too beautiful to live in'.

Nevertheless, the view is splendid – given clear conditions. Great End is nine miles away, so you could be peering through a lot of Lakeland haze.

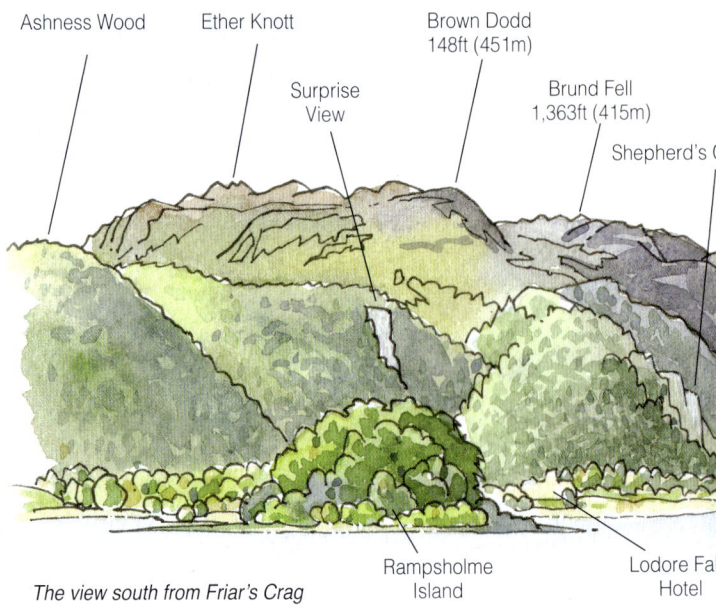

Friar's Crag

The view south from Friar's Crag

Ashness Wood
Ether Knott
Surprise View
Brown Dodd 148ft (451m)
Brund Fell 1,363ft (415m)
Shepherd's C
Rampsholme Island
Lodore Fal Hotel

Derwent Island & Skiddaw
The house and island are strictly private

Derwent Island became a sanctuary for German miners in 1565, when they were badly received by the locals. In the 18th century the eccentric Joseph Pocklington built a house and various follies on the island. The Marshall family lived here for over a century, handing ownership to the National Trust in 1951.

Rampsholme Island once had a bloomery for smelting iron ore, while St Herbert's Island is named after the 7th-century hermit immortalised by Wordsworth. Derwent Water even has a 'ghost' island, rising from the lake bed on a cushion of marsh gas near Lodore. Believe it when you see it!

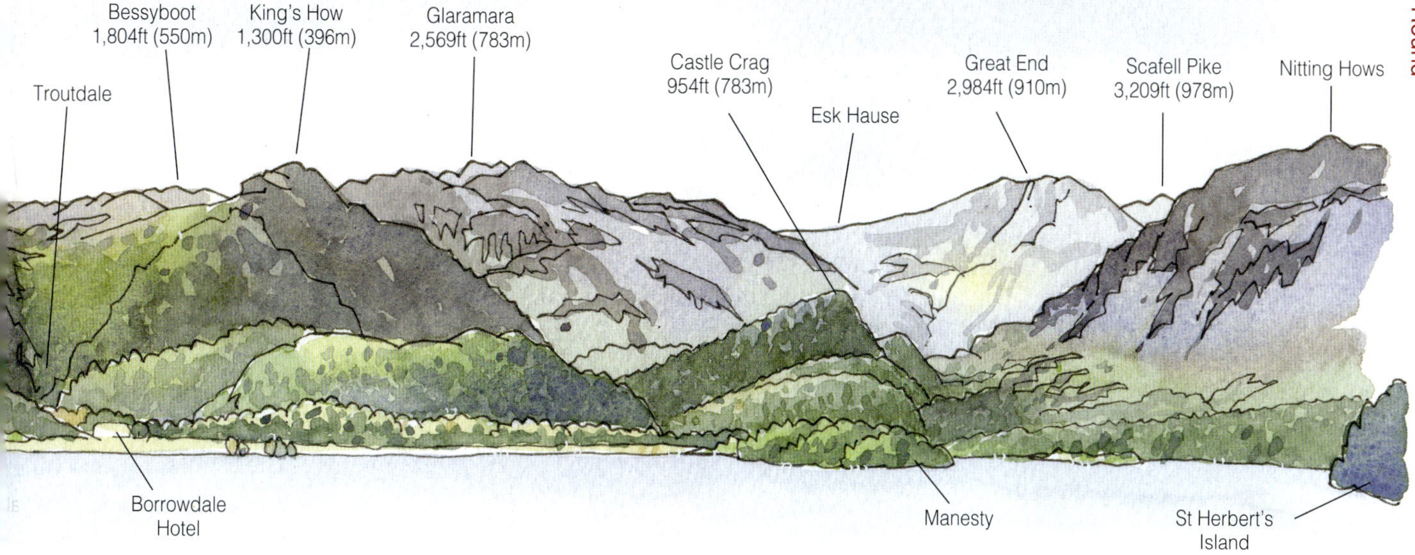

Bessyboot 1,804ft (550m)
King's How 1,300ft (396m)
Glaramara 2,569ft (783m)
Castle Crag 954ft (783m)
Esk Hause
Great End 2,984ft (910m)
Scafell Pike 3,209ft (978m)
Nitting Hows
Troutdale
Borrowdale Hotel
Manesty
St Herbert's Island

Derwent Water & Buttermere Round

13

1 Derwent Water & Buttermere Round

 ## The Tour

Leave Keswick on the A5289 Borrowdale Road. Soon Derwent Water can be glimpsed between the trees on your right, while Walla Crag towers above the road on your left. There are a couple of lakeside car parks where you can pause and admire the views of Cat Bells across the water.

After two miles or so you have the choice of making a detour to Watendlath. It's around five miles there and back along a narrow single track road with passing places. Apart from some stupendous views, you will visit the Lakeland icons of Ashness Bridge, Surprise View and Watendlath tarn itself.

Turn off the lakeside road, just beyond the Ashness Gate launch landing stage, onto a steep hill signed Ashness Bridge & Watendlath. A steady ascent through light woodland brings you to an open fellside and Ashness Bridge, the famous packhorse bridge over Barrow Beck. Cross to park in the wood on your right.

Continue along the winding road through more woodland to Surprise View, where there's another handy car park and a lofty view across the lake that's always a wonderful surprise.

After another mile or so cross a cattle grid into a narrow open valley with Watendlath at its head. Stone walls and fences edge the narrow road and passing oncoming vehicles requires precise manoeuvring and patience.

Return along the single road and at the lakeside junction turn sharp left back onto the B5289 Borrowdale Road.

A mile of twisting road through woodland brings you to the head of the lake and the magnificent state-of-the-art Lodore Falls Hotel.

Ashness Bridge

14

Watendlath

Watendlath Tarn

Lodore Falls Hotel enjoys a sylvan position at the foot of Gowder Crag

This moorland hamlet nestles at the head of a Lake District 'hanging valley', 600ft above the surface of Derwent Water. The tiny tarn, packhorse bridge and a huddle of farm buildings are one of the most photographed compositions in Lakeland.

Sir Hugh Walpole, who lived across the lake at Brackenburn and is buried in St John's churchyard, Keswick, set his 'Herris Chronicle' books here.

Justifiably a magnet for tourists, Watendlath should be avoided on summer bank holidays. One way to avoid the crowds is to leave your car at Surprise View car park and walk along the east side of the river. Watendlath has a car park, toilets and a small tea garden, which usually closes in winter.

PIT STOP
Lodore Falls Hotel

Most stylish in the area. A £13m spa annex opened in 2019 with 18 cavernous suites, treatment rooms, hydrotherapy pool, steam rooms, saunas and a champagne bar. It joins Mizu, a pan-Asian restaurant in the main building, serving sashimi, veggie nigiri and fiery Thai green curry. Sophisticated splendour with prices to match. Parking.

To access the falls walk through the spa gardens and cross a footbridge. Only worthwhile if there's been heavy rain. It does happen. *lakedistricthotels.net/lodorefalls*

1

Derwent Water & Buttermere Round

High Lodore Farm Cafè

 Further south along the B5289 you come to High Lodore Farm Café, sheltered beneath Shepherds Crag, and the Borrowdale Hotel in an equally attractive setting. Soon after you reach another Lakeland favourite, the double-arched bridge at Grange-in-Borrowdale. We shall return to Grange later in the tour.

The road now follows the twists and turns of the River Derwent as tree-covered cliffs close in, forming the aptly-named 'Jaws of Borrowdale'. Lakeland walker's guru Alfred Wainwright, called this area 'the loveliest square mile in Lakeland'.

There's a car park off a sweeping bend from where you can stroll to the Bowder Stone, a huge rock as big as a house that has intrigued visitors since Victorian times.

After a final twist or two the road clears the woodland and the aspect widens to reveal the distant village of Rosthwaite across water meadows. Look out for the marker posts along the roadside indicating the depth of floodwater. Rain – and floods – are no strangers to Borrowdale.

The Bowder Stone

The Bowder Stone is an immense block, some 30ft high by 60ft long, and weighing around 2,000 tons. It rests on a narrow crest like a keel of a chunky ship and seems likely to roll over at any moment but has stood firm since it was dumped here thousands of years ago by an Ice Age glacier.

The rock was established as a tourist attraction by the wealthy and eccentric Joseph Pocklington in 1798. He'd already built a house on Derwent Island where he staged mock invasions and firework displays as part of the Derwent Water Regatta. Let loose on the Bowder Stone he constructed a 'crazy ladder' so tourists could stand on the summit. He also built a cottage by the rock as a home for an old woman to 'lend the place quaint atmosphere'.

The ladder tradition has been maintained and in 2019 the National Trust proudly installed the latest in a series of ladders onto the top. This one is of metal and, unlike Pocklington's, conforms to all modern safety standards.

Grange Bridge

Rosthwaite

Surrounded by craggy and colourful fells, their lower slopes swathed in trees, Rosthwaite stands between two lively rivers at the centre of Borrowdale's flat valley floor. A wonderful setting.

There's also more to Rosthwaite than first meets the eye. The main road has to squeeze between buildings and negotiate an awkward bend past the Scafell Hotel before continuing up the valley. The village itself lies away from this road, a place of infinite nooks and crannies, whitewashed cottages and comfy lodging places. There's also a car park (which fills quickly) and toilets down a side road at the village hall.

The River Derwent flows along the western side of the village from its source on the fells above Seathwaite at the head of Borrowdale. Stonethwaite Beck sweeps past buildings on the eastern side after tumbling down from steep-sided Langstrath. Stake Pass at its head is the walker's route into Langdale.

Borrowdale Hotel

The village bottleneck

A popular walk starts from here to Castle Crag, the 'rotten tooth' prominent in the Jaws of Borrowdale and once the site of an Iron Age fort. The sensational all-round views from the summit are rich reward for the short but steep and rocky climb, partly through the ancient detritus of an abandoned slate quarry.

The two-mile route over the fell to Watendlath is also a favourite family walk.

Yew Tree Farm. The tea room is in a former farm building opposite

PIT STOPS

High Lodore Farm Café (Shepherd's Café)
Homemade cakes, soup and quiche. Plenty of outdoor seating and parking. Great views. *highlodorefarm.co.uk*

Borrowdale Hotel
Luxurious former coaching inn. Afternoon teas and locally sourced dinners with traditional silver service. Parking. *lakedistricthotels.net/borrowdalehotel*

Flock-in Tea Room, Yew Tree Farm, Rosthwaite
Extensive menu with tasty Herdwick pasties and stews made from meat raised on the farm. Car park nearby. Terrific views. *borrowdaleyewtreefarm.co.uk*

Derwent Water & Buttermere Round

17

Our route continues to Seatoller, launch pad for the ascent of Honister Pass into Buttermere. Narrow and bendy, the pass snakes alongside the beck with up to 25% gradient in places. The steepest parts are less than a mile in length each side with a similar stretch across the summit plateau. Here the barren landscape is 'enlivened' by the Slate Mine buildings and their garish signs The pass drops dramatically into Buttermere, following the lively Gatesgarthdale Beck that dances between huge rocks and boulders fallen from the heights of Fleetwith Pike above.

The road levels out approaching the Gatesgarth car park at the head of the lake. Enjoy the fantastic views as the road snakes around the lakeside but keep a look out for pedestrians (walkers and sheep).

Seatoller

The road to Honister Pass

This hamlet was once the service area for a regular stagecoach service over Honister Pass. It only ceased in 1934 when the road was properly surfaced and the horses' hooves could no longer grip the termac surface.

These days the attractive cluster of farms and B&B establishments boasts a large car park and toilets, so provides an excellent base for walkers.

The road to Seathwaite

The Borrowdale road continues past Seatoller to the head of the valley at Seathwaite, the legendry wettest inhabited place in England. Around 140in of rain falls on the tiny settlement in an average year. In September 1966, it was hit by five inches of rain in one hour! During four days in November 2009, almost 20in fell, roughly equivalent to ten months average rainfall in London. Storm Desmond also brought devastation in 2015.

This part of Borrowdale is also famous for the discovery of plumbago (graphite) which was mined on the slopes of Base Brown during the 16th century. A pure form of carbon, it had many uses, including being a vital ingredient in the casting of cannon balls, which made it so valuable it could only be transported under armed guard. The mines established the Keswick pencil industry, but the yield from Borrowdale gradually diminished and the last mine closed in 1836.

The Buttermere side of the pass

The mine centre entrance

Honister Pass

With gradients of one in four and an altitude of 1,167ft, Honister Pass is one of the steepest and highest in the region. The light green slate mined at Honister since the late 1600s is thought to be around 450 million years old. It's still seen in local walls, on rooftops and as highly-polished table tops or gift shop momentoes.

By 1890 production at the mine had reached 3,000 tons a year and more than 100 men were employed in often appalling conditions underground. In those days the mine was so isolated miners lived there during the working week and messages to the company offices in Keswick were sent by carrier pigeon.

Business gradually declined and by the 1980s a complete shutdown was threatened. However, in 1997 the mine was reopened by new owners, Bill Taylor and Mark Weir, as a tourist attraction. Some inspired entrepreneurship transformed the site into one of the district's major adventure centres and Honister Slate (or more correctly Westmorland Green Slate) is back in commercial production. Mark Weir was killed in 2011 when his helicopter crashed near the mine.

ATTRACTION

Honister Slate Mine

England's last working slate mine, offering underground tours and several different climbing routes. These include the exhilarating Via Ferrata following the original miner's route across the exposed face of Fleetwith Pike using a fixed cableway, ladders and supports.

If that's not scary enough, try the 'Infinity Bridge', the longest wire bridge in the country, which crosses a yawning 2,000ft chasm and is so called because you can't see the end when it's misty. You need to book in advance and unsurprisingly the bridge crossing is weather dependent.

There's a 'walker's' car park on the site, at a fixed price of £5 for all day, refundable if you spend more than £10 in the shop or take part in one of the adventure activities. *honister.com*

PIT STOP

Sky Hi Café

Part of Honister Slate Mine visitor centre. Wholesome, locally-sourced grub: pies, bacon butties, soup. The name refers to its location (the highest in Lakeland) and not necessarily the parking fee for a pop-in coffee. *honister.com*

1

Derwentwater & Buttermere Round

The head of Buttermere

The tiny Church of St James was built on a rocky perch at the foot of Newlands Pass in 1840. Twin bells hang in the bell turret and the wrought iron porch gate depicts a hill shepherd and his sheep. A stone tablet set into the window sill of a south window is a memorial to Alfred Wainwright, the famous walker and author of guidebooks. The window looks out on his favourite place to walk, Haystacks, where at his wish his ashes were scattered.

At the junction with Newlands Hause

Details of Buttermere village are in Tour 2 but this one turns sharply right before then, at the church, signed Keswick. Climb Newlands Hause, snaking between the smooth hillsides of Whiteless Pike and High Snockrigg. At the summit (1,093ft/333m) there's a small car park from where you can admire Moss Force waterfall, and a distant view of Blencathra in the northern skyline. Continue for three and a half miles of delight down Newlands valley, where the aspect gradually changes from barren fellsides to soft Beatrix Potter-type country of green fields, white farmhouses and sheep. There's also a great view of the west face of Cat Bells.

Newlands

Considering how close it is to major tourist centres, Newlands is a surprisingly tranquil and unspoilt gem. What little roads there are go nowhere in particular, which all adds to the attraction. Little Town is said to be the inspiration for Beatrix Potter's *The Tale of Mrs Tiggy Winkle* and her sketches include places around the dale.

The valley was extensively mined and quarried for many centuries, with lead, copper, silver and even gold being extracted. The Goldscope Mine, which closed at the end of the 19th century, yielded such large amounts of lead and copper that it was called 'Gottesgab' (God's Gift) by the German miners who helped develop it.

Newlands from the Hause

1

Derwentwater & Buttermere Round

When you come to a Y-junction, take the right leg, signed 'Stair'. It's a compact hamlet with a tight packhorse bridge over Newlands Beck. Further on the Swinside Inn soon appears, spread prominently across a wooded hillside.

The road continues to wind attractively though light woodland to another Y-junction. Take the right leg, signed 'Grange', heading for the northern end of Cat Bells. Drive up the hill and go left, negotiating a tight hairpin bend, also signed 'Grange'. When you clear the trees a sensational view across Derwent Water appears. A mile of double yellow lines prohibits parking on the roadside, but there are a few laybys that you may be lucky enough to find vacant. Skiddaw and Blencathra dominate the skyline in the north.

The road continues through woodland, winding past 'Brackenburn', once the home of author Sir Hugh Walpole. A series of cosy small hotels and B&B establishments line the approach to Grange. There's parking in the village – but not a lot!

Cross the bridge over the Derwent and turn left for the four miles back to Keswick and the end of this tour.

Causey Pike 2,090ft (637m)

Stair

Swinside Inn   **PIT STOP**
Traditional, atmospheric, family run, dog friendly pub with bed and breakfast rooms above. Large outside area to admire the view of Newlands – and pheasants running free in the fields! Parking. *swinsideinn.co.uk*

Swinside Inn

Manesty Park

22

Brandlehow Bay

Grange

Furness Abbey established the hamlet of Grange-in-Borrowdale in the 14th century to administer its local affairs in the valley. Beautifully situated where the River Derwent widens, so a stone bridge, built in 1675, requires two graceful arches to cross. The water is remarkably clear, enhancing the colours of the smooth stones in the riverbed to perfection.

Attractively slate-built and genteel, modern Grange marks its ecclesiastical past by having both a Methodist Chapel by the bridge and a lovely church, Holy Trinity, built in 1860 with churchyard walls of slate slabs set on end.

These days Grange continues to look after local affairs by catering for the multitudes of tourists who pass daily along its single narrow street.

Grange Café

Grange Café   PIT STOP
Simple traditional snacks, sandwiches, cakes and homemade soups. Exceptional breakfasts. Sells the unusual Borrowdale Honey. Situated in the centre of the village. Outdoor seating with gorgeous views.

Sir Hugh Walpole (1884-1941)

Brackenburn

Born the Bishop of Edinburgh's son in New Zealand, Hugh Walpole later divided his time between Borrowdale and London. He wrote 42 novels, most famously the Herries quintet, which has a Lakeland setting. Brackenburn, built in 1909, was bought on first sight in 1923. Walpole extended the house several times so he could still see the lake over growing trees. His wide-windowed study is above the garage. Visitors are not admitted.

Central Grange

TOUR 2
Braithwaite, Newlands and Whinlatter Round • 24 miles
Braithwaite – Newlands – Buttermere – Crummock Water – Loweswater – Lorton – Whinlatter Pass – Braithwaite

Beginning at the village of Braithwaite, this route heads south through the unspoilt Newlands valley, climbing steadily to the head of Newlands Hause where you can pause at a small car park to admire the fell and valley views. A steep descent down the hause brings you to Buttermere village, where there's several attractive pit stops. You might also fancy the four-mile walk around the lake to really appreciate the grandeur of this majestic valley.

After appreciating Crummock Water's quiet dignity there's a short detour to Loweswater village for more terrific views. Loweswater, the third of this tour's differing trio of lakes, is one of the hidden gems of the area.

Returning to the Cockermouth road and continuing north takes you to the peaceful two-part village of Lorton. The big finish is crossing Whinlatter Pass, climbing through the forest back to Braithwaite, after perhaps calling at the visitor centre or the aptly named Cottage in the Wood for refreshment.

There's a variety of pitstops along the route and some of the most spectacular scenery this part of the Lakes can offer.

Braithwaite

The cheery village of Braithwaite nestles at the foot of the Whinlatter Pass with a magnificent mountain backdrop of Grisedale, Causey Pike, High Stile and Barrow, forming the famous Coledale Horseshoe as it curves round the head of Coledale Hause. Set within the horseshoe, the village seems almost to have been pushed into it like a wedge.

Coledale Beck winds its way down the valley and enters a narrow gorge before tumbling and rushing through the village where it's crossed by two humped backed bridges aptly named High Bridge and Low Bridge.

Coledale Beck and Low Bridge at the centre of the village

The village shop and the road to Newlands Valley

Braithwaite's superb location has always attracted visitors and it's now very much a holiday village with a large caravan and camping site and the whole gamut of accommodation on offer. There used to be a railway station on the other side of the A66, part of the much lamented Penrith to Workington line. It opened in 1864 and was dismantled in 1972 after the Beeching restructuring of the railway network in the 1960s.

Across the valley the magnificent bulk and classic mountain sculpture of Skiddaw is seen full on, making a colourful and dramatic sight. Here guest houses line the hillsides like boxes at the opera.

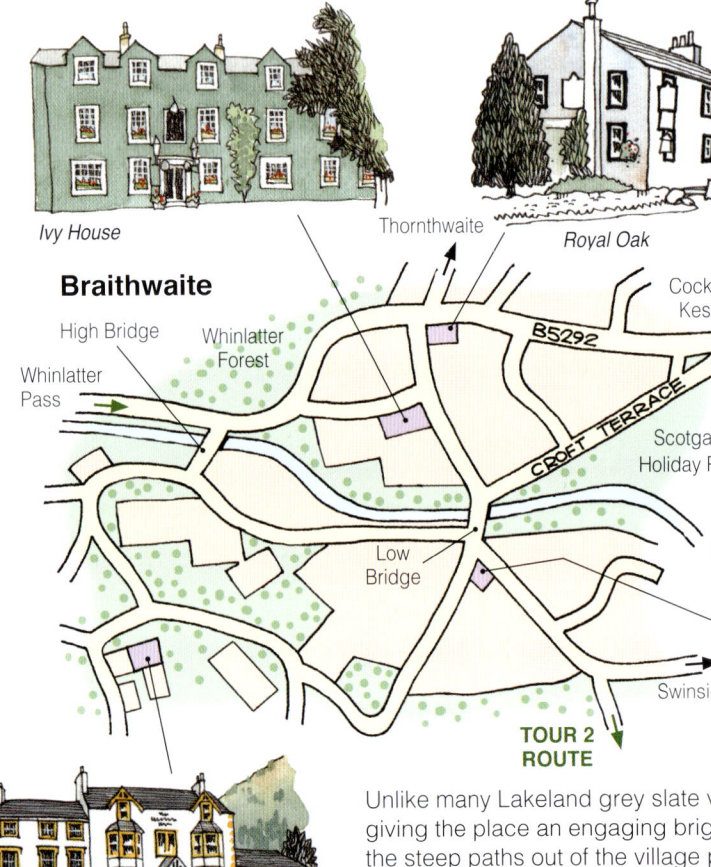

Braithwaite, Newlands & Whinnatter Round

PIT STOPS

Royal Oak
Traditional country inn with ten en-suite bedrooms, roaring fires in winter and plenty of outdoor seating for summer months. Oak beams and hearty pub grub served in the bar or restaurant. Packed lunches for walkers. *royaloak-braithwaite.co.uk*

Coledale Inn
More an upmarket hotel than a drop-in restaurant, but a wonderful hill top situation. There's 20 en-suite rooms, a beer garden and bar meals. Built in 1824 as a woollen mill, then became a pencil mill, eventually acquiring licensed premises status. Full of Victorian prints, furnishings and antiques. *coledale-inn.co.uk*

Ivy House
Cosy cottage style dining, serving succulent Lakeland classics to modern European delicacies with a menu changing daily. Completely renovated after the 2015 floods
honestlawyerrestaurant.co.uk/ivy-house-restaurant

Village shop Groceries, off licence, newspapers. Hot and cold snacks, cakes and ice cream. Open every day except Christmas.
braithwaitegeneralstore.co.uk

Unlike many Lakeland grey slate villages most of the houses at Braithwaite are painted white, giving the place an engaging bright and cheerful appearance. There's some great walks up the steep paths out of the village past the Coledale Inn with fabulous views across the rooftops.

Braithwaite is pleasant enough and has everything holiday makers need but nobody seems to hang around the village for long. They're all going somewhere else. Many to climb the beckoning fells but some – like us – will be driving up the Newlands Valley to Buttermere.

 ## The Tour

Leave Braithwaite on the road by the shop signed 'Newlands & Buttermere'. Narrow and bendy, it climbs out of the village past some desirable houses. At a fork in the road bear right. Beyond some light woodland the aspect opens to reveal inviting views of Newlands Valley ahead.

Cross a cattle grid onto an unfenced road running alongside the steep side of Barrow. Pass the junction going off left to Stair and begin the three and a half miles climb up Newlands Hause. There are places to park as the narrow road climbs steadily and the landscape grows more spartan. Most of the farms along the way offer accommodation. At the summit there's a small car park with extensive fell views all round.

The descent to Buttermere ends at the church at the bottom of the hause where you turn right to Buttermere village and the car parks.

Newlands Valley was covered in Tour 1 but this time we travel in the opposite direction. The experience is always different when the mountain landscape fills your windscreen rather than being restricted to reflections in small driving mirrors.

Rising to around 1,093ft (333m), Newlands Hause is the most prominent of the numerous minor roads which criss-cross this enchanting valley. It's not the most challenging of the Lakeland passes but snaking across the eastern flanks of Barrow, Causey Pike and Knott Rigg it's a great viewpoint for Cat Bells, Maiden Moor and Robinson across the valley. The Buttermere side is steeper, sweeping down across the northern side of High Snockrigg with the great bulk of Whiteless Pike dominant across the deep gully of Sail Beck. Moss Force waterfall is a short walk across the fellside from the car park on the summit.

The cattle grid

Birkrigg Cottage in Newlands that featured in the BBC TV series 'The A Word'

Approaching the summit and Moss Force

The Buttermere descent

2 Buttermere

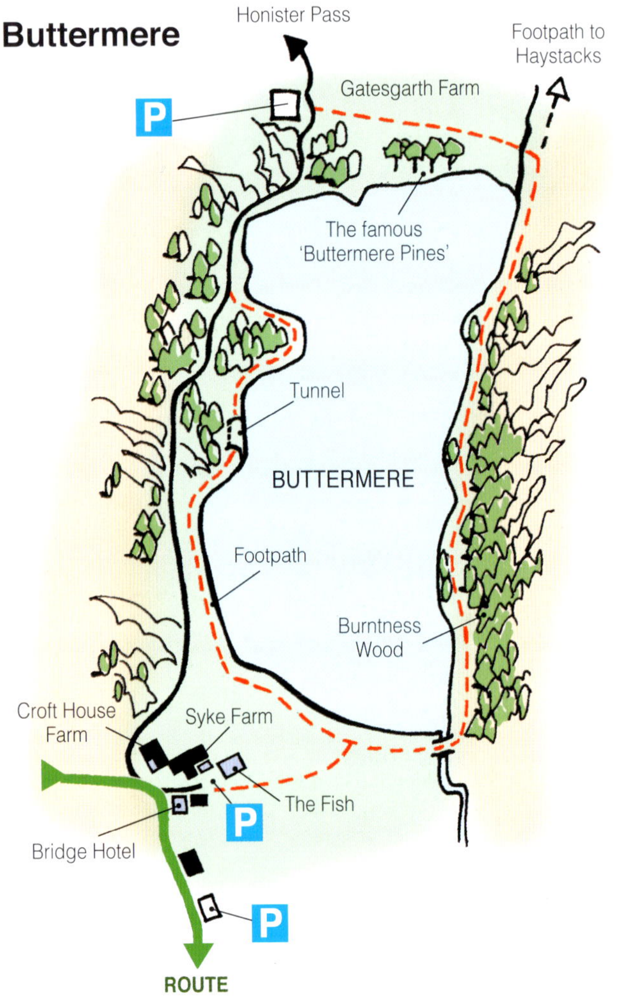

The Buttermere valley is around eight miles long, running north-west from high ground around Great Gable down to the flat meadows of Lorton. There are three lakes – Buttermere, Crummock Water and, just off the main valley, Loweswater – strung together like jewels on a necklace of rivers. The small village of Buttermere lies between the two southernmost lakes.

The lake is only a mile and a quarter long and less than half a mile wide, though at 75ft maximum it is deep by Cumbrian standards. Lack of organic material keeps the water very clear, while sediment from Honister Slate Quarry enhances the magnificent reflections with a unique greenish quality. The scenery is also special with the rugged 2,000ft (610m) high ramparts of the High Stile range towering over the lake. Buttermere has many fine fells but they're no match for these awesome neighbours.

A popular family walk goes around the lake starting from the Buttermere or Gatesgarth car parks. Part of the route goes through a tunnel dug by gardeners at nearby Hassness House to allegedly give them something to do during the winter.

Crummock Water and the head of Buttermere

The 'Maid of Buttermere'

The tabloids of the time went into overdrive in 1802 when Mary Robinson, the daughter of the landlord of the Fish Inn (now simply 'The Fish'), was tricked into marriage by a dastardly conman and bigamist calling himself the Honourable Alexander Hope. He was unmasked by the local gentry, tried for franking his mail as a bogus MP and hanged at Carlisle a year later.

Mary, 'The Maid of Buttermere', had plays and songs written about her – even Wordsworth mentioned the scandal in his *Prelude* – and visitors flocked to the Fish to catch a glimpse of the unfortunate girl. More recently, in 1987, Melvyn Bragg wrote a novel based on her story.

Mary later married a Caldbeck farmer, led a relatively contented life raising four children and died in 1837.

The Fish   **PIT STOP**
Good traditional food, ales and ambiance. Loved by walkers, climbers, and real ale enthusiasts. Parking. *fishinnbuttermere.co.uk*

PIT STOPS

Croft House Farm Café
Fresh sandwiches, Panini and bagettes plus scones, cakes and traybakes. Open every day except Christmas. *crofthousefarmcafe.co.uk*

Syke Farm Tearoom
Traditional farmhouse-style food with a variety of homemade cakes and scrumptious lunches. Also the best ice cream in the district, made with milk from the cows grazing in the meadows below the farm. Parking outside.

Bridge Hotel
Dog-friendly hotel with 21 en-suite bedrooms and six self-catering apartments. Their USP is that none of the rooms have TVs, radios or wifi to 'maintain the rural tranquility'. Rear bar for hungry walkers. Parking. *bridge-hotel.com*

The Buttermere Valley from Low Bank

 Leave Buttermere village on the single road heading north. A short walk up the fellside opposite a car park on the village outskirts rewards you with a terrific view along the valley.

A half mile or so further on brings you to Crummock Water. The road runs along the attractive but rather spartan lakeside, where there are a few places to park. The headland of Rannerdale Knotts thrusts its rocky headland, Hause Point, into the lake and after rounding this obstacle the road turns away from the lake into farmland.

Grasmoor rises along the east side of the road and there are a few parking places (often filled by the vehicles of people making an ascent). A final gentle climb brings you to a layby at a small wood from where you can look back across the lake to the remarkable mountainscape you are leaving behind – but there will be more!

The view south from Brackenthwaite

Crummock Water

At two and a half miles long, less than a mile wide and 144 feet deep, Crummock Water is larger than Buttermere but a lot less busy.

A narrow, half-mile strip of farmland separates the two lakes, which suggests they were probably one long stretch of water way back in the ancient geological past. The southern end shares some of Buttermere's high crags but in the north, Grasmoor and Melbreak take over.

Buttermere and Loweswater flow into Crummock and it's also fed by numerous streams including the beck from Scale Force, which at 170 feet high is Lakeland's tallest waterfall. The River Cocker begins here, flowing towards Cockermouth where it joins the River Derwent and occasionally floods the town.

31

2

Almost a mile further on, turn sharp left at a junction signed Loweswater 1½ miles. Loweswater village is a scattered hamlet that confusingly overlooks Crummock Water rather than the lake of that name. Pause on the hillside at the village hall to take in the classic view across Crummock Water to Grasmoor and Mellbreak. Just down the hill is the village pub, the Kirkstile Inn, which is almost as famous and well-regarded as the view.

Continue to Loweswater lake, less than a mile away. The road runs along the side of the lake and there's a small car park at the end where you can turn around.

Return to the junction with the road from Crummock Water and continue through one the lushest and prettiest parts of the northern Lakes to the village of Lorton.

Loweswater

This is a lake for lovers of peace and tranquility, who savour the gentle four-mile stroll around the shores after a heavy Sunday lunch.

Loweswater is one of the region's smallest, shallowest and least-known lakes. Its uniqueness lies in the fact that it's the only lake whose waters flow towards the centre of the Lake District (actually into Crummock Water) rather than towards the sea.

It's just over a mile long, not quite a mile across and has an average depth of around 60ft, which makes it one of the first lakes to freeze over in winter. Loweswater is undoubtably pretty but it's the seclusion so close to tourist hot-spots that makes it so appealing.

PIT STOP
Kirkstile Inn
Welcoming 16th-century hostelry with beams and country furnishings. Serves quality bar meals including local trout and fell-bred steaks, and their own award-winning craft beers. Enjoy a glass of Loweswater Gold in the beer garden while watching the sunset over Mellbreak. Eleven rooms to let.
kirkstile.com

Kirkstile Inn and Mellbreak

Lorton

This scattered village is really two, High Lorton and Low Lorton, neither of which have an obvious centre. With a pretty church, picturesque old houses and some interesting historical artifacts, a stroll round the peaceful streets is always worth while. Lorton was an agricultural settlement until the 19th century, then enjoyed a prosperous period in the textile industry and is now largely a commuter and holiday village.

Cottages Dating to the early 1800s and once part of the original Jennings Brewery buildings.

Lorton Hall The estate dates to 1663. The manor house has a pele tower and is strictly private.

Village Hall Former malthouse of the original Jennings Brewery, established in 1828. The company moved to a larger site at Cockermouth in 1874.

PIT STOPS

The Barn Tearoom
Situated a mile south of Lorton this country house boasts five attractive rooms and a tearoom that serves meals and snacks all day. Immaculate 15-acre grounds make this a popular venue for weddings. The tearoom closes when there's an event on.
newhouse-farm.com

Lorton Village Shop
Also known as 'The Shed With A View', this admirable enterprise is packed with local and ethical items, ranging from food, coffee and crafts to hiker's and cyclist's supplies. It supports over 80 local businesses and has become an unmissable tourist attraction.
lortonvillageshop.co.uk

Wheatsheaf Inn
Lorton's 17th-century local pub serves substantial bar meals with Jennings Ales. There's a beer garden and a large camping and caravan site at the back.
wheatsheafinnlorton.co.uk

The Lorton Yew
Immortalised in a poem by William Wordsworth. Soon after, a storm reduced the tree's 27ft girth to a mere 13ft. At least 1,000 years old, the yew still stands, now on private land.

The Barn Tearoom

Leave High Lorton on the B5292 signed Keswick and with a fine view of the Buttermere fells across the fields on your right, climb steadily for a couple of miles into Whinlatter Forest. The Forest Centre is located at the highest point (1,000ft/305m). As you begin to descend look out for the pretty Cottage in the Wood that can be a surprise in this setting, but is exactly as the name suggests. Don't miss the layby with the view of Skiddaw across the Bassenthwaite flood plain. The descent then steepens until a sharp left turn returns you to Braithwaite village and the end of the tour.

Climbing Whinlatter Pass

Whinlatter Forest Park
ATTRACTION

England's only true mountain forest, planted in response to timber shortages following World War One, Whinlatter now encompasses 4.6 sq miles of pine, larch and spruce.

It's home to all mannner of outdoor activities, with nine walking trails, three cycling routes, play areas and way-marked running tracks. There's also Go Ape, a high wire adventure course featuring rope bridges, tarzan swings and zip slides 40ft up in the treetops – the highest in the country.

Inside the Forest Centre there's seasonal exhibitions on the area's wildlfe, and during the nesting season (Easter to August) you can watch the wild ospreys at Bassenthwaite on a live video nest-cam link.

The first 20 minutes parking is free, then up to an hour for £2.20. All day is £8. Note the main car park is 'pay on exit', which raises the barrier.

Silkins Café
PIT STOP

Part of the Forest Centre. The alpine-style café serves hot and cold meals, sweet treats and proper coffee. An outdoor terrace overlooks the forest and the valley down to Derwent Water. *forestryengland.uk/whinlatter*

Silkins Café

As Lakeland passes go Whinlatter is not particularly high, just managing to exceed 1,000 feet. For much of the way the outlook is restricted by trees, but a mile out of Braithwaite there's a clearing which enables a panoramic view of Skiddaw and Bassenthwaite. Derwent Water is just out of sight on the right. In particularly wet periods it's not uncommon for the flatlands between the two lakes to flood, turning them into a single huge stretch of water.

Though of lowly stature, Binsey has the distinction of being the most northern 'Wainwright' fell. Beyond it there are no more Lakeland hills, only the coastal plain and the Solway Firth.

Cottage in the Wood

PIT STOP
Cottage in the Wood
Restored 17th-century restaurant with rooms and a string of awards. Included in many 'Best of' lists and guides. Contemporary decor and locally-sourced food including Herdwick Hogget, West Cumbria coast seafood and wild ingredients foraged from the surrounding forest.
thecottageinthewood.co.uk

Skiddaw and Bassenthwaite Lake from Whinlatter Pass

Binsey 1,467ft (447m)
Bassenthwaite Lake
Ullock Pike 2,270ft (692m)
Long Side 2,408ft (734m)
Dodd 1,647ft (502m)
Skiddaw 3,054ft (931m)
Carl Side 2,448ft (746m)
South top
Carsleddam
Skiddaw Little Man 2,838ft (865m)
Jenkin Hill
Lonscale Fell 2,345ft (715m)

35

TOUR 3

Grasmere to Bassenthwaite • 25 miles

Grasmere – Dunmail Raise – Thirlmere – Keswick bypass – Braithwaite – Bassenthwaite Lake – Bassenthwaite village

PETROL
Keswick
Ambleside
PodPoint charging station at Grasmere

Wythburn Church and Helvellyn

The Lake District National Park is crossed by two main roads. Around 24 miles of the A66 goes west from Penrith to Bassenthwaite, while the A591, voted Britain's most popular road, runs for 28 miles north from Kendal to Carlisle. This tour includes sections on both highways. Beginning at Grasmere, the busiest village in the park, it ends at Bassenthwaite, one of the most peaceful.

Three prominent lakes are visited, including Thirlmere, which once was two, Leatheswater and Brackmere, until the valley was flooded in 1897 to provide water for a thirsty Manchester. This part of the Lakeland road network was severly damaged by Storm Desmond in 2015. The road along the west side of Thirlmere and the one through St John's in the Vale remain closed. A three-mile stretch of the A591 at the southern end of the lake was closed for six months, reopening to vehicular traffic in May 2016.

From chocolate-box Grasmere the route climbs over Dunmail Raise to the more rugged landscape of the north. Beyond Thirlmere you're into big fell country with great views of Blencathra and Skiddaw. We skirt Keswick to join the A66 and cross the spectacular concrete bridge over the gorge of the River Greta.

Soon we reach Bassenthwaite, one of the most enigmatic of the Lakes, and leave the busy A66 for the peaceful and often overlooked countryside north of the lake. Our tour ends snuggled up to Skiddaw in Bassenthwaite, prettier than Grasmere village and nowhere near as busy!

The Grasmere location looking north

enterprise. Hotels, gift shops and cafés abound. Grasmere is an unabashed tourist village.

The River Rothay meanders around the buildings and an inspired footpath follows it linking two car parks, one at either end of the village.

The romantic popularisation of Grasmere began with the Lake Poets, particularly with the village's most famous literary lion, William Wordsworth. He was a true Cumbrian, born at Cockermouth in 1770, schooled at Hawkshead and resident of the Rothay valley in various houses for over 50 years until his death in 1850.

The Wordsworth Museum at Town End draws tourists and serious scholars from all over the world, and the £3m Wordsworth Trust Research Centre dedicated to the study of Wordsworth and British Romanticism opened nearby in 2005.

Bridge over the Rothay near the church

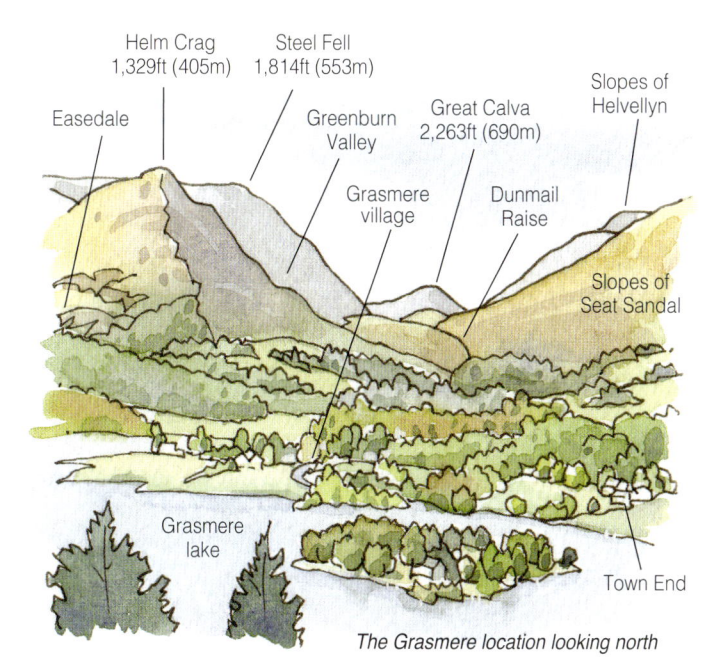

The best-known, most visited, and most revered of all the Lakeland villages, Grasmere sits regally in a lush bowl of fells, overlooked in the north by Helm Crag and edged by the pretty lake in the south that shares the village name.

Grasmere village is never going to rival its surroundings in a beauty contest, but it's pleasant enough for a major tourist honeypot. Most of the grey slate buildings are 19th or early 20th century and the delightfully unstructured street plan gives the village an endearing old-fashioned look. However, at street level most places are given over to some kind of commercial

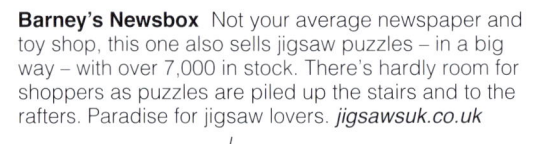

Barney's Newsbox Not your average newspaper and toy shop, this one also sells jigsaw puzzles – in a big way – with over 7,000 in stock. There's hardly room for shoppers as puzzles are piled up the stairs and to the rafters. Paradise for jigsaw lovers. *jigsawsuk.co.uk*

Grasmere

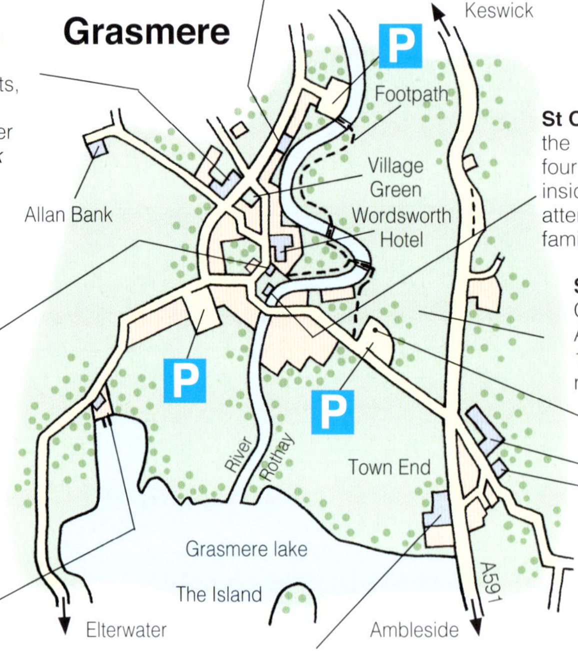

Heaton Cooper Studio Showcase for the much admired lakeland artist, William Heaton Cooper (1903-95) and his talented family. Originals, prints, general art books and a superb art materials shop. The splendid Mathilde's Café is named after William's Norwegian mother. *heatoncooper.co.uk*

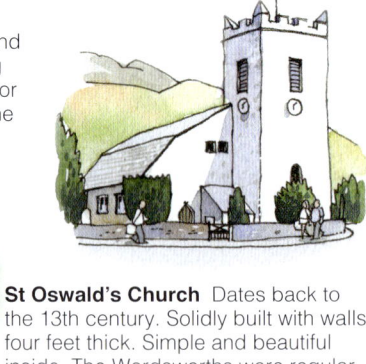

St Oswald's Church Dates back to the 13th century. Solidly built with walls four feet thick. Simple and beautiful inside. The Wordsworths were regular attenders and fifteen of the extended family are buried in the churchyard.

Sports ground Site of the famous Grasmere Sports held in late August almost every year since 1868. Events include wrestling, fell races, hound trails and dog shows.

POD Point Charging Station

Wordsworth Museum Unrivalled collection of some 70,000 manuscripts, first editions, books, letters portraits and personal items of the family. Shop, café and small car park.

Gingerbread Shop Built in 1882 as the village school, it was let to Sarah Nelson in 1854 who first made the hard and spicy Grasmere Gingerbread here. The business survives but the recipe remains a closely guarded secret.

Faeryland The archiaic spelling is 'to accentuate the natural magic of this place'. As if anywhere on the shores of Grasmere needed any help! It's actually a lovely little tea garden where you can hire rowing boats, feed the ducks and sample a huge range of loose leaf teas from around the world. *faeryland.co.uk*

Daffodil Hotel A recent makeover of this huge, grey slate Victorian-era hotel places it amongst the best of the village's boutique establishments, but after years as *The Prince of Wales* the desire for a Wordsworth connection has saddled it with a rather wimpy new name.

Dove Cottage Wordsworth shrine and pilgrimage centre for tourists and scholars. Lovingly cared for and hardly changed since the poet's day, despite the thousands of visitors traipsing through. Gets very, very busy.

The Wordsworth Houses

William Wordsworth and his sister, Dorothy, moved into Dove Cottage, a former inn, in 1799. He married Mary Hutchinson in 1802, a childhood friend who bore him five children. With a frequent flow of friends, including fellow Lake Poets, Coleridge and Southey, the tiny seven-roomed cottage often became severly overcrowded.

After eight happy years, during which William wrote his greatest works, they relocated to Allan Bank, a large house on the lower slopes of Helm Crag. William disliked the house and referred to it as a 'temple of abomination', so two years later they moved to the parsonage in the village. It was another unhappy move and two of the the Wordsworth children, Thomas (aged six) and Catherine (three) died here. Mortified, the family left Grasmere in 1813 for Rydal Mount, two miles away.

Dove Cottage (1799-1808)

Allan Bank has had several refurbishments since Wordsworth's time including a transformation to Victorian Gothic Revival style during the 19th century. It was later owned by Canon Rawnsley, co-founder of the National Trust, who bequeathed it to the organisation in 1920. The house lay neglected for decades and after a huge fire in 2011 the Trust decided that it should be restored and opened to the public.

When the doors were eventually opened in 2012 the house was still unfurnished and undecorated, and confused visitors were invited to suggest what to do with the place. It's a handsome house in a terrific location but the future of Allan Bank still seems to be shrouded in uncertainty.

The parsonage, opposite the church in Grasmere, is now home to the vicar of St Oswald's and isn't open to the public.

The Parsonage (1811-13)

Allan Bank (1808-11)

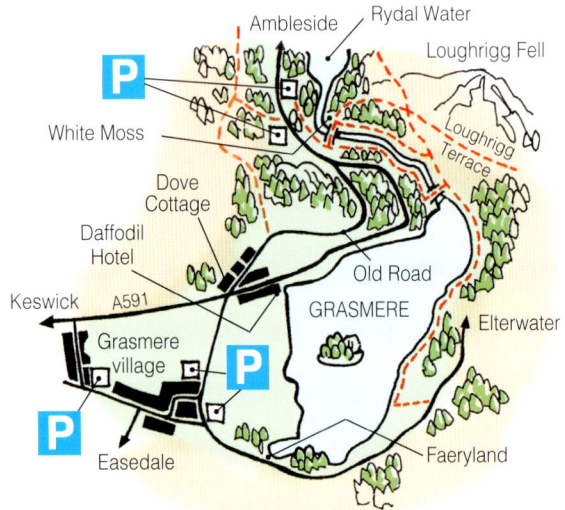

PIT STOPS

This is only a random selection from the huge variety available in the village.

The Jumble Room
Highly-rated, relaxed dining. Local cuisine, Asian, International, vegetarian friendly, vegan options.
t*he*jumbleroom.co.uk

Tweedies Bar
Grasmere's nearest thing to an upmarket gastro-pub. Part of the Dale Lodge Hotel on Langdale Road. Stone-flagged floors, wood burner stove and Large beer garden. Very popular.
dalelodgehotel.co.uk

Mathilde's Café
Part of the Heaton Cooper Studio so must be good. Quick bites. Delicious Scandinavian food. Vegetarian friendly.
heatoncooper.co.uk/mathildes-cafe

Wordsworth Signature Restaurant
Award-winning fine dining in a luxury hotel at the village centre. Organic spa and 38 *en-suite* rooms. Formally The Earl of Cadogan's shooting lodge.
thewordsworthhotel.co.uk

Lucia's Coffee & Bakehouse
Small but perfectly formed. Huge range of freshly-baked goodies. Takeaway shop. By the bookshop on the green.

Grasmere lake

Grasmere is one of the area's smaller lakes being only around one mile long, a half-mile wide, with a maximum depth of 70ft. A weir at the outlet to Rydal Water maintains the water level. The wooded island on the lake is known simply as 'The Island', a rather prosaic name for a place so rich in poetic romanticism. A stone shelter on the isle was built for grazing sheep. Apart from the Daffodil Hotel at Town End there are no buildings at the lakeside.

The A591 follows the northern bank but the lake is unseen from the village and you have to walk along the back road to Elterwater to appreciate all its glory. Set against low wooded fells in their autumnal colours or when a morning mist hangs over the water, the scene can be very glorious indeed.

Parts of the lakeshore are private, so it's not possible to walk all the way round the lake, though you can walk along the Elterwater road then join a footpath down to the lake and on to White Moss. Return to the village along the elevated old road along the west side of the lake with splendid views.

Faeryland and the boat landings

The Tour

Leave Grasmere heading north on the A591. Pass the Macdonald Swan Hotel on the outskirts of the village and, as the road begins to rise, the Traveller's Rest inn. While climbing Dunmail Raise look to Helm Crag on your left where rocks on the summit form the silhouette of the famous 'Lion and the Lamb', as pointed out to passengers by generations of coach drivers. There's a short stretch of dual carriageway across the top of the Raise, then a meander down the northern fellside to the woods around Thirlmere.

Dunmail Raise

Rising to only 781ft (238m) and around two miles long, calling the Raise a 'pass' would be an elevation to an unmerited level. However, it does represent a significant cultural and topographical divide between north and south Lakeland. Some say (usually northerners) that the south is soft and chocolate-box, while others (southerners) consider the north to be a wild and untamed wilderness.

The Raise, an ancient routeway since the Stone Age, is named after Dunmail, the last Norse King of Cumbria, who was defeated in battle on this hillside in AD945 by the combined forces of the Saxon King Edmund I and Malcolm, King of the Scots. Legend has it that Dunmail was killed in the battle and Cumbrians taken prisoner were forced to collect rocks and pile them on his body, forming a cairn. Other Dunmail warriors fled with the Crown of Cumberland, climbing to Grisedale Tarn below Helvellyn where they threw it into the depths to be safe until the king would rise again to lead them.

A pile of stones still graces the summit of the Raise and the king has yet to reappear, but the story was scuppered when an unromantic history geek observed that Dunmail actually lived for another thirty years after the battle!

Macdonald Swan Hotel

Traveller's Rest

The 'Lion & the Lamb'

PIT STOPS

Macdonald Swan Hotel
Upmarket hotel with a homely atmosphere and a Walkers' Bar for weary hikers and their dogs. Gleaming white, it was popular in Wordsworth's day, but not by William who disliked strong drink and white buildings, though he did mention the Swan in his epic poem, *The Wagonner*. *macdonaldhotels.co.uk*

Traveller's Rest, Grasmere
An original 16th-century coaching inn with all the trimmings: oak beams and inglenooks, log fires and a beer garden with views. The bar-restaurant serves award-winning food while another bar features local real ales. Ten letting rooms with en-suites.
lakedistrictinns.co.uk/travellers-rest

Beyond a hump-backed bridge, the aspect widens to reveal Thirlmere and the tree-clad lower slopes of Helvellyn rearing dramatically on your right. The road twists for a couple of miles along the lakeside to The Swirls, where there's a layby on your left and a more substantial car park on your right. It's worth stopping here to admire the view across the lake and north along the valley to Blencathra. There's often an ice cream van in the layby too.

Continue through fields crisscrossed by stone walls to the King's Head, a former coaching inn at the scattered hamlet of Thirlspot. Further along, the main road swings left as a minor road goes off right, the B5322 signed Threlkeld. This goes through the delectable St John's in the Vale, a beautiful and varied 'short cut' to the A66. Sadly this road fell victim to Storm Desmond in 2015 and is still closed, but you can still see the great slab of Castle Rock from the A591. It so inspired Sir Walter Scott in 1813 that he wrote 'The Bridal of Triermain', his romantic narrative-poem celebrating the exploits of a Knight errant, Sir Roland De Vaux.

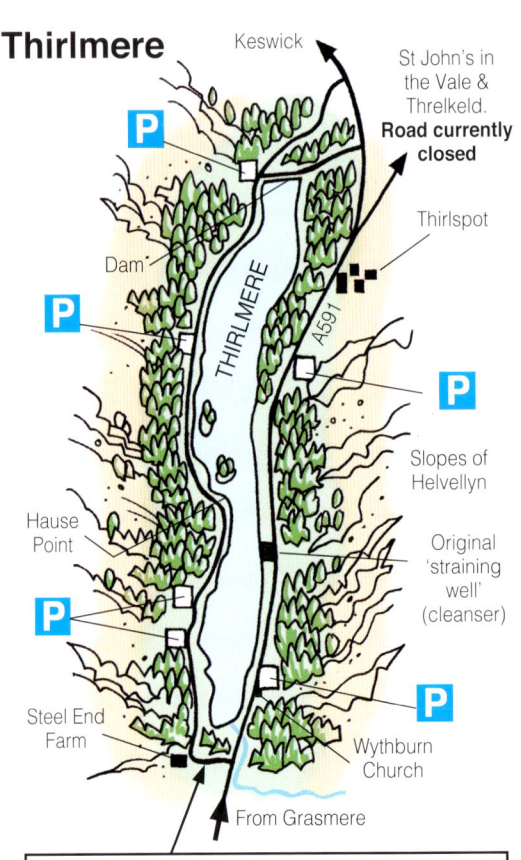

Note The road along the western side of the lake was severely damaged by Storm Desmond in 2015 and is still closed.

Though often overlooked in the pantheon of Lakeland picturesque on the grounds that it was created by human endeavor and thus 'unnatural', Thirlmere is worth attention as the only significant stretch of water with the mighty Helvellyn range as a backdrop. It's also a superb example of Victorian civil engineering.

Thirlmere was created from two smaller lakes – Leathes Water and Wythburn Water – by the construction of a dam during 1890-94 to supply water to the city of Manchester via a 100-mile aqueduct. The first pipeline, a single 40in-diameter pipe, was established in 1897, when the lake level was raised to 20ft above normal. As the demand for water increased so did the number of pipes. By 1927 there were four and the water level had been raised to 50ft above normal. A plan to add a fifth pipe was shelved and water is taken from Haweswater instead.

The Thirlmere Aqueduct is the longest gravity-fed aqueduct in the country with no pumps anywhere along its route. A tunnel was dug under Dunmail Raise by two teams working towards each other. The two tunnels met within 10in of centre.

Thirlmere is a little over three miles long and just under half a mile wide with a maximum depth of around 130ft. An outlet flows north down St John's Beck, joining the Gleneramackin at Threlkeld to become the Greta that flows through, and sometimes into, Keswick. Situated at the north end of the lake, the dam is 857ft long and 50ft thick at the bottom, rising 64ft above the old stream bed. The top is 18ft wide and has a road across it.

A crenelated building on the east side of the lake housed the original 'straining well' (a cleansing system) at the beginning of the tunnel under Dunmail Raise and is now a grade two listed building. It was made redundant by the installation of a water treatment plant at the southern exit of the tunnel at Grasmere, which began operation in 1980.

The old road and Steel End Farm, which escaped the flooding of the valley

Raven Crag from the dam

The lake, now owned by United Utilities, provides water for Keswick. The company is currently laying a pipeline to also take water from Thirlmere to West Cumbria. Due to be completed by 2022, this will enable the present extraction of water from Ennerdale Water to cease.

One of few buildings that survived the raising of the water level is the tiny church at Wythburn. Built in 1640, it was enlarged in 1872, but despite this is still claimed to be the smallest church in England. A pub, the Nag's Head, used to stand opposite, but fell victim to the flooding of the valley.

The fellsides around the lake were originally planted with 120 acres on conifers as an early cash crop, but the alien trees were widely disliked. Now, thanks to modern forestry management, Thirlmere has a more natural look.

3

Grasmere to Bassenthwaite

King's Head, Thirlspot

PIT STOP

In a fabulous location at the foot of Helvellyn, this 17th-century former coaching inn with 17 en-suite bedrooms also includes two highly-rated restaurants. The bar serves traditional favourites while the St John's Restaurant offers a creative four-course seasonal menu. *lakedistrictinns.co.uk/kings-head*

King's Head

Blease Fell · Gategill Fell · Blencathra 2,848ft (868m) · Hall's Fell · Slopes of High Fells · Castle Rock · High Rigg · Thirlspot · A591 road

St John's in the Vale from The Swirls car park

A further two miles brings you to Dale Bottom. Blencathra is in view as you climb Nest Brow, while the great bulk of Skiddaw makes an appearance straight ahead. The road levels out and Bassenthwaite Lake joins the magnificent panorama. There's a glimpse of Borrowdale on your left before you twist steeply down Chestnut Hill. Turn sharp right at a junction, signed Penrith & Workington, and climb to the A66 interchange.

Turn left at the first junction, signed Workington & Cockermouth, onto the high level bridge that curves over the River Greta. Latrigg, a lovely spur of the Skiddaw massif, is ahead and to the left, across the Keswick rooftops, there's a fine view of the Derwent Fells.

Greta Bridge and Clough Head

Greta Bridge Carries the A66 across the deep gorge of the River Greta. Built of concrete during 1974-77 and costing £1.5 million, the four-span structure was at the time one of the longest bridges of its type in the country. Despite furious criticism before and during construction, in 2000 it was voted the 'Concrete Structure of the Century' by the Concrete Society.

Robinson 2,147ft (654m)
High Stile 2,644ft (806m)
High Snockrigg 1,725ft (526m)
Red Pike 2,479ft (756m)
Newlands Valley
Knott Rigg
Rowling End 1,422ft (433m)
Ard Crags 1,860ft (567m)
Causey Pike 2,035ft (620m)
Crag Hill 2,749ft (838m)
Sail 2,530ft (771m)
Outerside 1,863ft (568m)
Barrowl 1,494ft (446m)
Grasmoor 2,791ft (851m)
Coledale Hause
Hopegill Head 2,525ft (770m)
Grisedale Pike 2,593ft (790m)
Keswick
Greta Bridge

The Derwent Fells from Storm's Farm

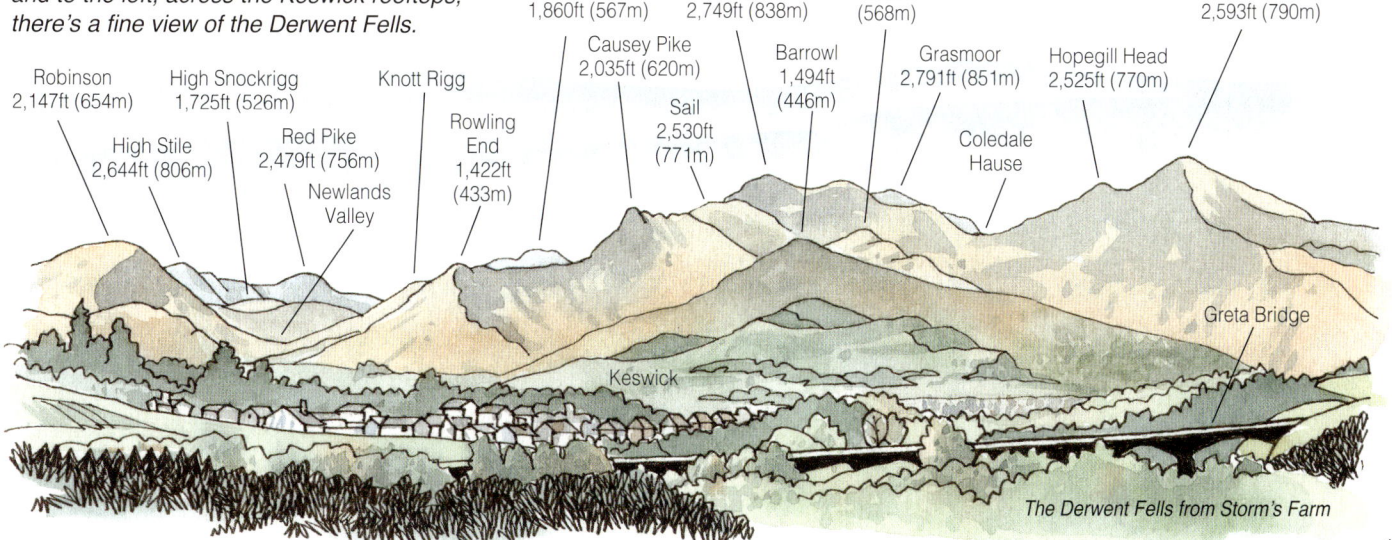

Bassenthwaite Lake

The broad and often busy road now descends for a mile or so to the large Crosthwaite Roundabout. Keep on the A66 ahead, signed Workington & Cockermouth, and the switchback of fells and wooded dales around Braithwaite are now revealed. Swinging right, the broad highway avoids the village and continues north alongside the tree-covered cliffs of Thornthwaite Forest. Bassenthwaite Lake is reached in another two miles or so, where there's a lay-by to pause and admire the exceptional views, especially that of Skiddaw across the water meadows. Continuing north, the road twists through a couple of miles of light woodland that includes a dual carriageway where the south side follows the route of the old railway line. Towards the end of this section, part of the old road turns off the A66 to the Pheasant Inn.

Beyond the woodland at the north end of the lake, turn right onto a minor road signed, Castle Inn & Dubwath B5291. This follows the lakeside to the stone Ouse Bridge over the River Derwent as it flows out of the lake to Cockermouth. Keep straight on for the Lakes Distillery, otherwise turn right, over the bridge, signed Castle Inn & Bothel, to continue along the lakeside. The Armathwaite Hall entrance and the road to the Lake District Wildlife Park are together on your left. A half mile or so further on brings you to the Castle Inn at crossroads on the A591 Carlisle to Keswick road.

Turn right, signed Bassenthwaite & Keswick, then after around 100 yards take the minor road on your left signed Bassenthwaite Village. Follow this typical north Lakeland country road, then turn right to cross a little stone bridge over Dash Beck into the village of Bassenthwaite and the end of this tour.

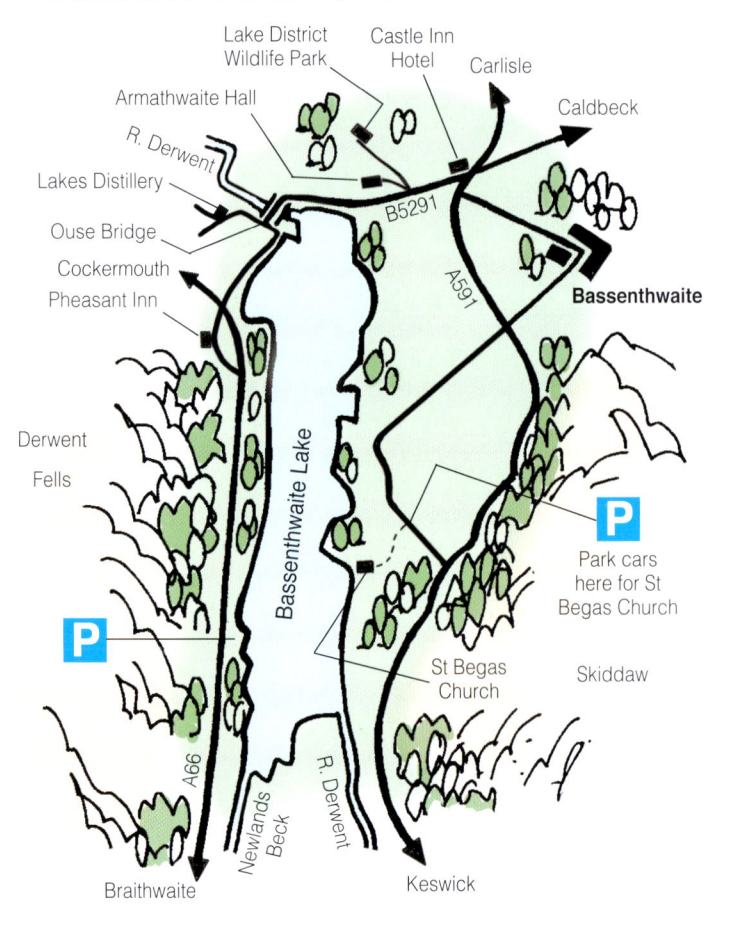

As local wags have it, Bassenthwaite Lake is actually the only true 'lake' in the Lake District. All the others are 'meres' or 'waters'. It's the most northerly of the lakes and at four miles long, just under a mile wide and with a maximum depth of 70ft, one of the largest.

Pheasant Inn

There's no real settlement at the lakeside so it's a peaceful outpost and, except for the heavy A66 traffic along the west side, relatively unspoilt. *The Guardian* newspaper named Bassenthwaite one of 'the best lakes to visit in Europe'.

Castle Inn Hotel

Lakes Distillery
ATTRACTION & PIT STOP

A short detour from Ouse Bridge takes you to Cumbria's first commercial distillery. Established in 2014, it now produces an own-brand whisky, vodka and gin using water from the River Derwent. There's hour-long tours, which round off with a tasting session, after which you might like to buy a bottle or three from the shop. An on-site bistro serves coffee and cake plus lunches, teas and supper, with a courtyard and attractive garden for *al-fresco* dining. *lakesdistillery.com*

PIT STOPS
Pheasant Inn
Upmarket accommodation and dining in a beautiful old coaching inn, set in peaceful woodland just off the main A66 on its very own layby. Preserved period bar and comfy lounges. Bistro serves classic bar meals.
the-pheasant.co.uk

Armathwaite Hall
One of the Lake District's most glamorous country-house hotels, a restored 16th-century mansion set in 400 acres of deer park and woodland. Open to non-residents for lunches, bar lunches, afternoon teas and dinner.
armathwaite-hall.com

Castle Inn Hotel
Luxury hotel with 45 comfortable bedrooms, four meeting rooms and leisure facilities, including an indoor heated swimming pool. The relaxed Castle Inn Tavern serves light meals and bites with Ritson's Restaurant catering for more formal dining.
castleinncumbria.co.uk

ATTRACTION
Lake District Wildlife Park
Over 100 species of wild and domestic animals roam free in this beautiful 24-acre park, with birds of prey flying displays, a picnic and play area, plus a café. Part of the Armathwaite Hall group.
lakedistrictwildlife park.co.uk

Armathwaite Hall

St Begas Church occupies an idyllic and isolated situation on the east shore of Bassenthwaite Lake and can only be reached on foot. Turn off the A591 into a narrow lane, signed Bassenthwaite Church ¾mile. Park in the layby and take a hard surfaced pathway across the fields to the church.

The building dates from about AD 950, though the site may be older, and was extensively restored in 1874. Christian worship has taken place here for over a thousand years and people travel from all over the world to sample its serene and mystical atmosphere. The church interior is beautifully maintained and always open.

Tennyson is said to have been moved to write his lines about Excalibur while staying nearby at Mirehouse and more recently Melvyn Bragg used St Begas as the setting for his Anglo-Celtic epic *Credo*.

An osprey

In 2001 a pair of ospreys nested near Bassenthwaite Lake, the first pair to do so for at least 150 years. Every year since, ospreys have made the 3,000-mile journey back from Africa to nest and raise their young. They usually arrive in April, the eggs hatch in June and then the adults and chicks head back to Africa in September.

The Lake District Osprey Project operates a viewpoint at the Forestry Commission's Dodd Wood, near Keswick, from where the nest can be viewed through high powered telescopes from a safe distance. You can also watch the birds on the nest-cam at Whinlatter Forest Centre

St Begas Church

Bassenthwaite village

With a green, a pub and ducks on the river flowing through it, Bassenthwaite is the archetypal English village. But this being the Lake District, there's also three farms within the village itself and many of the houses are barn conversions, holiday lets or second homes. An avenue of fine trees across a green make a grand entrance from the south and a stroll around the maze of narrow streets is a excellent way to work up a thirst for a drink at the Sun Inn.

Snuggled up against the north side of Skiddaw and with the dramatic ridge of Ullock Pike soaring almost from the village streets, Bassenthwaite has plenty to enjoy.

Sun Inn

PIT STOP

Sun Inn
This 16th-century inn wears its age well with oak beams, log fires, real ales and quality bar meals. Dog-friendly for friendly dogs. There's a large car park and a sensational view to Ullock Pike and Skiddaw from the outside seating area.
suninnbassenthwaite.co.uk

Central Bassenthwaite

TOUR 4
The Langdales • 15 miles

Grasmere – Elterwater – Chapel Style – Great Langdale – Dungeon Ghyll – Blea Tarn – Little Langdale – Skelwith Bridge – Ambleside

This is a journey of contrasts between the two Langdale valleys. As the name suggests, Great Langdale is rugged and monumental, the flashy mountain sculptures at its head topped by the peerless Langdale Pikes. Great Langdale Beck winds across the valley floor feeding, at the lower end, Elterwater lake. The lake is basically three tarns which expand with the rainfall, but it's undoubtedly pretty and there's a hard surface path to it from Elterwater village.

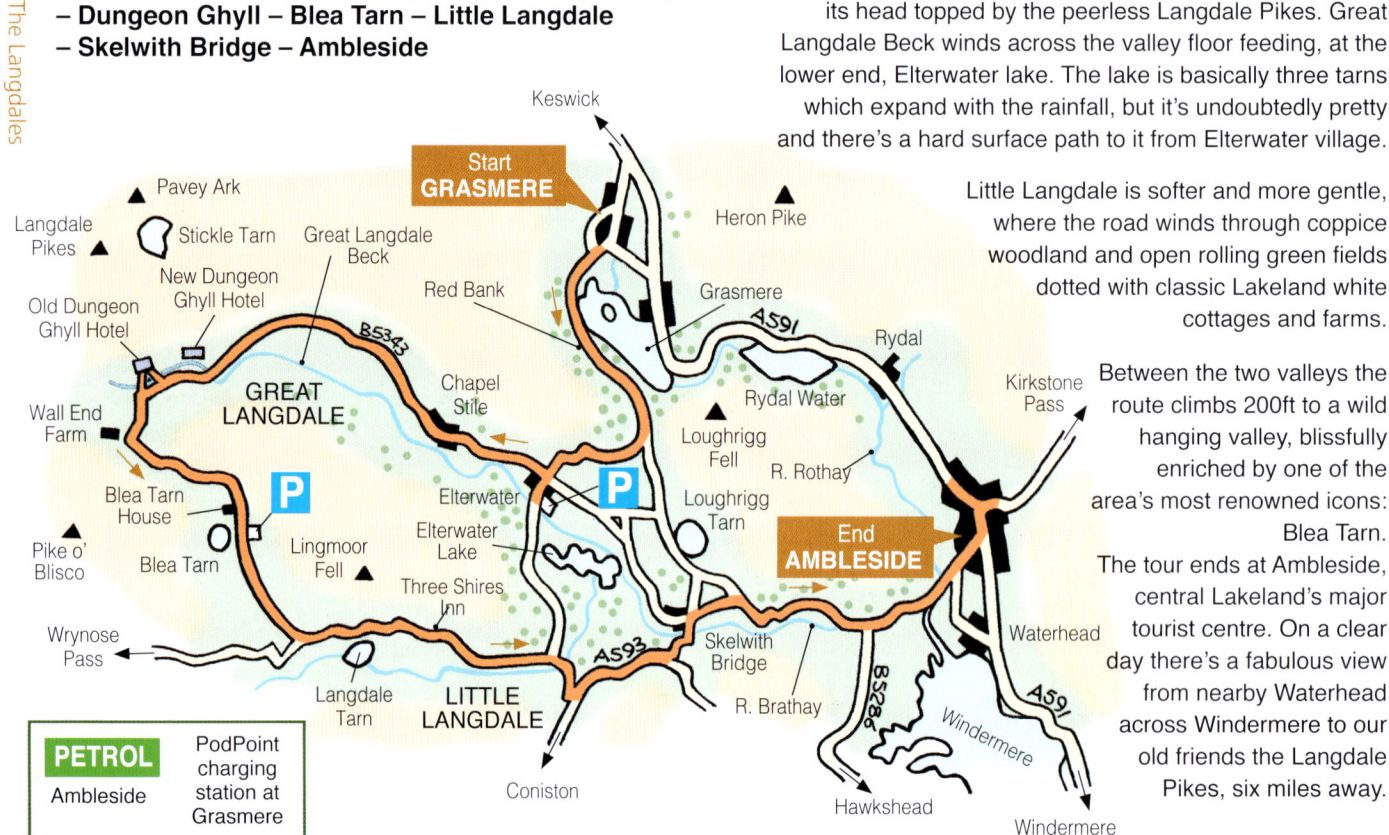

Little Langdale is softer and more gentle, where the road winds through coppice woodland and open rolling green fields dotted with classic Lakeland white cottages and farms.

Between the two valleys the route climbs 200ft to a wild hanging valley, blissfully enriched by one of the area's most renowned icons: Blea Tarn. The tour ends at Ambleside, central Lakeland's major tourist centre. On a clear day there's a fabulous view from nearby Waterhead across Windermere to our old friends the Langdale Pikes, six miles away.

Start: GRASMERE
End: AMBLESIDE

PETROL Ambleside
PodPoint charging station at Grasmere

The Tour

Leave Grasmere on the narrow back road to Elterwater. When you enter dark woodland lookout for walkers, who have to use the road to reach the footpath down to the lakeside. The route steepens as you pass some fine hillside houses, discreetly screened by trees. Climbing across the side of Red Bank provides some elevated views through the woodland to the lake. The final steep section (25% in places) brings you to a Y-junction. Take the narrow right leg, signed Langdales & YHA on a stone at the roadside.

Twist behind the YHA building, and as the road exits the trees a fabulous view across Elterwater Common to the Langdale Pikes is revealed. Pause or park where you can to savour this exceptional panorama. The road continues to twist downhill until the turn off to the centre of Elterwater village at the bottom.

The back road from Grasmere

- Little Langdale
- Wetherlam 2,502ft (763m)
- Swirl How 2,637ft (804m)
- Great Carrs 2,585ft (788m)
- Elterwater village
- Lingmoor Fell 1,540ft (469m)
- Oakhow Crag
- Great Langdale
- Crinkle Crags 2,818ft (859m)
- Bowfell 2,949ft (902m)
- Esk Pike 2,903ft (885m)
- Gimmer Crag
- Loft Crag 2,238ft (682m)
- Thorn Crag
- Harrison Stickle 2,415ft (736m)

The view across Elterwater Common to Great Langdale

4 Elterwater

Sitting serenely at the entrance to Great Langdale, the riverside village of Elterwater has an industrial history totally at odds with today's tranquil character. The cluster of cottages, built of green slate from nearby quarries, gather around one of the prettiest village greens in Lakeland with the Britannia Inn at its head, and a magnificent maple tree shading a circular wooden seat. It's an idyllic spot, always busy with walkers, photographers and aimless untethered sheep.

Elterwater is now totally tourism based with, it's said, only a quarter of the houses permanently occupied. The rest are holiday homes.

Elterwater Green and the Britannia Inn

Elterwater village

Britannia Inn
PIT STOP

Family run on Elterwater's green and hugely popular with hikers and travellers. The 17th-century oak-beamed restaurant was originally a gentleman's farmhouse. Fresh, rustic and seasonal pub dining with daily changing specials and a separate lunch and dinner menu. Nine cosy rooms for hire.
thebritanniainn.com

4 The Langdales

In the past, the principal industries at Elterwater have been farming, quarrying for slate and gunpowder manufacture. The first two activities continue, while evidence of the latter survives in the grounds of the Langdale Estate, a holiday development founded in the 1930s and redeveloped as a timeshare in the 1980s.

Slate quarrying was well established in the area by the end of the 18th century. In 1824, quarry owners converted an old bark mill in the village into a gunpowder factory. Local juniper wood was used in the manufacturing process. Eighteen waterwheels provided power and up to 90 people were employed. A cannon was regularly fired to test the product.

When demand lessened the works were closed in 1920 and the buildings demolished. The site was opened as a time share estate in 1981. Quarrying is still carried on in the hills behind the village.

Former quarryworkers' cottages

4
The Langdales

Elterwater lake is just over a half mile long, with a width that varies hugely with the rainfall, and a maximum depth of about 20 feet. Compared to the other grander lakes it can be a disappointment.

Even calling it a lake may be pushing it a bit, but the three tarns and their soggy surroundings do act as a holding point for the massive volume of water that flows down the valley from the huge collection area in the dalehead fells. Without it the lower valley and Ambleside would suffer even more flooding than they do now. After rain Elterwater can double in size and has risen as much as five feet in a night.

Despite its position in the minor league of lakes, only Elterwater can boast a backdrop of the Langdale Pikes, so it has a lot going for it.

Elterwater lake and the Langdale Pikes

An excellent hard-surfaced footpath runs from the village to the lake, then follows the River Brathay to Skelwith Bridge. Skelwith Force on the river is relatively low in height (about 17 feet) but water is forced through a narrow gap making an impressive (and noisy) fall, especially after rain.

A thousand years or so ago Norwegians settled in the valley, followed by whooper swans, also from the far north, that they named the lake Heltrewatre, 'the lake of the swans'. The swans are still regular winter migrants from Siberia.

Much of the lowland around Elterwater was once swamp until being bought up (along with several of the farms) by an enterprising local, John Harden, in 1820. He deepened the lake and drained the marshes, creating the landscape of bumps and hillocks seen today. In the 1830s he sold back the reclaimed land to various local farmers – at a handsome profit, no doubt. The precise ownership of the lake is unclear these days, but it's still largely in private hands.

Leave Elterwater on the road from the Brittania Inn, signed Great Langdale. Turn left at the common onto the main valley road. Pass the Langdale Holiday Village. After a half mile or so swing right past Wainwrights' Inn into the small village of Chapel Stile. You can park behind the Co-operative Store and Brambles Café.

Chapel Stile

Like Elterwater, Chapel Stile owes its existence to the local slate quarries, some dating back to the 18th century. In those days Chapel Stile was known simply as Langdale Chapel. Holy Trinity Church was built into the fellside in 1857 to replace a chapel of 1750. A contemporary account records that it was in a sorry state of repair, with the pulpit collapsing while the clergyman was giving a sermon.

Apart from a few eyesores the village is untainted by modern developments, though, some of its facilities have disappeared or changed. Not so long ago the village had a post office with petrol pumps. Even the Wainwrights' Inn has seen service as a farmhouse, gunpowder factory manager's house, petrol station and hotel.

Wainwrights' Inn

Co-operative Store

PIT STOPS

Brambles Café
Situated on the top floor of the village Co-operative store, established in 1884. Serves big breakfasts, sandwiches and lunch. There's also picnic packs for walkers and flasks can be filled with tea or coffee. The ground floor sells groceries with gifts, walking and cycling equipment. Groceries can be pre-ordered for pick up when visitors arrive.
langdalecooperative.co.uk

Wainwrights' Inn
Welcoming slate-floored village pub with open fires, local beers and popular bar meals. Specialities are hot and cold delicious meats, fish & cheeses cooked in a smokehouse behind the pub. The name has no connection with Wainwright the fell walker. Wainwrights' (the position of the apostrophe after the 's' is significant) refers to wagon-builders at the nearby quarries. Alfred Wainwright was teetotal and disliked pubs.
langdale.co.uk/wainwrights-inn

4 The Langdales

4

The Langdales

Lakeland dry stone walls edge the narrow road as it heads west into the broadening valley with the Langdale Pikes growing in magnificence ahead. A couple of miles brings you to Dungeon Ghyll where there's two large car parks and a plethora of fine fell views. The Old Dungeon Ghyll Hotel is a half mile further up the valley, just off the main road.

The magnificent Langdale Pikes dominate the valley, their famous profile unmistakeable from miles around. They're not the highest peaks in the area but possibly own their dominence to their individual shapes, close grouping and isolation from other peaks. There is generally considered to be three of them: Pavey Ark, Harrison Stickle and Pike o' Stickle, though Loft Crag and Thorn Crag are sometimes added to the grouping. Pike o' Stickle, was declared a 5,000 year old axe factory in 1947 when Neolithic stone axe heads were discovered in a gully.

The Pikes are undoubtably the star attraction but the fabulous amphitheatre of mountains arrayed across the head of the valley are equally worthy of attention. Here, Great Langdale divides into two parts: Oxendale, where the narrow road climbs over to Little Langdale, and Mickleden, a barren highway for walkers taking the Stake Pass route into Borrowdale.

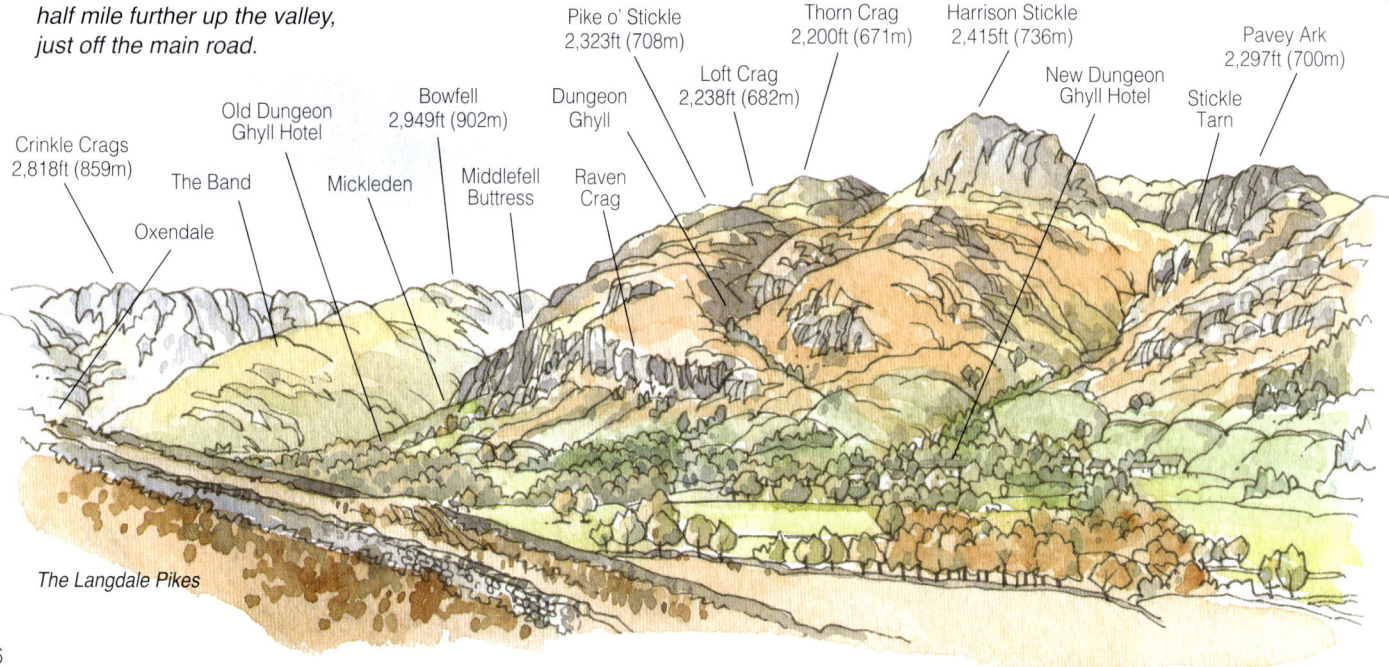

Pike o' Stickle 2,323ft (708m)
Thorn Crag 2,200ft (671m)
Harrison Stickle 2,415ft (736m)
Pavey Ark 2,297ft (700m)
Loft Crag 2,238ft (682m)
New Dungeon Ghyll Hotel
Stickle Tarn
Bowfell 2,949ft (902m)
Dungeon Ghyll
Old Dungeon Ghyll Hotel
Middlefell Buttress
Raven Crag
Crinkle Crags 2,818ft (859m)
The Band
Mickleden
Oxendale

The Langdale Pikes

A popular walk from Dungeon Ghyll is the steep climb up Stickle Ghyll to Stickle Tarn, dammed in 1838 to maintain a head of water for the Elterwater Gunpowder Factory. The well-trodden path follows a tumbling beck, interrupted at two-thirds height by a cascade that after fine weather can be quite spectacular.

At the top, Stickle Tarn is set in a scene of rocky splendour. The huge bastion of Pavey Ark looms over it, darkening the still waters of the tarn with a sombre reflection.

Jack's Rake, a curious slanting terrace, crosses Pavey Ark, running diagonally from bottom right to top left. It's a popular climb for adventurous fell walkers, but a dangerous place for anyone else. Even Wainwright couldn't face it for many years.

Slopes of Harrison Stickle — Pavey Ark — Tarn Crag — Stickle Ghyll — Stickle Tarn — Waterfalls

Sticklebarn Tavern

Stickle Ghyll

New Dungeon Ghyll Hotel

Old Dungeon Ghyll hotel

PIT STOPS

New Dungeon Ghyll Hotel
Most modern of the two Dungeon Ghyll hotels, built 1861 on the site of a medieval settlement. All 22 bedrooms are *en-suite*. There's a decent restaurant and Walker's Bar that serves meals. The outside terrace has terrific views *dungeon-ghyll.com*

Sticklebarn Tavern
A National Trust pub with a sunny slate terrace. Dogs on leads and muddy boots on owners are welcome inside and out. Real ale, good wine and locally sourced, planet-friendly food. *nationaltrust.org.uk/sticklebarn-and-the-langdales*

Old Dungeon Ghyll Hotel
Over 300 years old, well-worn, comfortable and a mite old-fashioned. Just as the clientele like it. Vintage oak furniture, comfy armchairs, open fires. The 12 country-style bedrooms don't even have TVs. Everyone's welcome for coffee and cake or hearty casseroles in the stone-flagged and lively Hiker's Bar, once the old cow stalls. There's live music most Wednesday evenings (acoustic only, naturally). Unrivalled position with challenging rock climbs right outside the back door. *odg.co.uk*

4 The Langdales

4

The Langdales

The route turns sharply left opposite the Old Hotel and crosses the valley to a cattle grid near Wall End Farm, the most remote of the Great Langdale settlements. The narrow but open road now begins to climb steeply alongside a babbling stream (if there's been no recent rain). The fell views are magnificent and the view back to The Langdale Pikes breathtaking. There are gentle hairpin bends to negotiate, but towards the top of the ascent there are places to stop and take in the magnificent scenery.

You're now in the hanging valley between the two Langdale valleys, a gift left by a generous primeval glacier. Cross a cattle grid with the bright streak of Blea Tarn shining in the distance. The narrow road (rough in places) meanders, with passing places, along the side of the valley to a listed 17th-century farmhouse, Blea Tarn House, the only building in the valley. Beyond it you soon reach the car park at Blea Tarn, where a walk down a track to the waterside is almost obligatory.

Resuming the tour, cross a cattle grid by the car park and soon Little Langdale valley appears ahead. Descend to join the road from Wrynose Pass (see tour 7). Turn left, signed Little Langdale and Ambleside. Stone walls hem in the narrow road but you do get a glimpse of Little Langdale Tarn, usually little more than an overgrown puddle.

Castle How

As you descend into Little Langdale look out for Castle How, a curious stepped knoll behind Fell Foot Farm in the valley. Protected by forts, a Roman road from Ambleside to Ravenglass once ran through here. It was later used by Viking invaders and historians have suggested that this draughty outcrop may have been the site of their annual parliament.

Blea Tarn House

Blea Tarn and the Langdale Pikes – one of the most photographed compositions in the Lake District

After the full-on magnificence of Great Langdale, Little Langdale, pretty though it is, can seem a little bland. Beyond the Three Shires Inn pass through mixed woodland, then climb steeply around a tricky Z-bend and turn left onto the A593, main Ambleside to Coniston road.

A mile or so brings you to Skelwith Bridge. Cross the stone bridge and, if you can find somewhere to park, stop for a while to enjoy this delightful riverside spot. Rejoin the Ambleside road for a pleasant three miles or so into the town and the end of this tour.

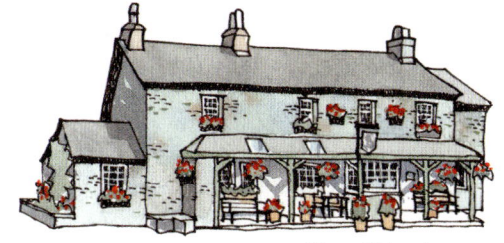

Three Shires Inn

Little Langdale is a restful gem of a valley, a half hidden world accessible only by narrow roads, protected in the west by a steep pass through the mountains and to the east screened from the busy world by thick woods. The River Brathay is the outflow of Elterwater, joining the River Rothay at Ambleside to flow on into Windermere. It's quite broad at Skelwith Bridge and can be feisty enough after rain to attact white water canoeists. Skelwith Force, modest in height but loud in volume, is just upstream and worth seeking out.

PIT STOPS

Three Shires Inn
A ten-bedroomed inn strategically located with views across the valley to Wetherlam and near the meeting point of the old counties of Cumberland, Westmorland and Lancashire (hence the name). Traditional Lake District food served in the restaurant and bar.
threeshiresinn.co.uk

Chesters by the River
This stylish bakery-restaurant cooks its own cakes, pastries and puddings daily and serves superior breakfasts and lunches. They also have a take-away option. Lovely terrace overlooks the river. The interesting shop next door sells upmarket crafts, gifts and books.
chestersbytheriver.co.uk

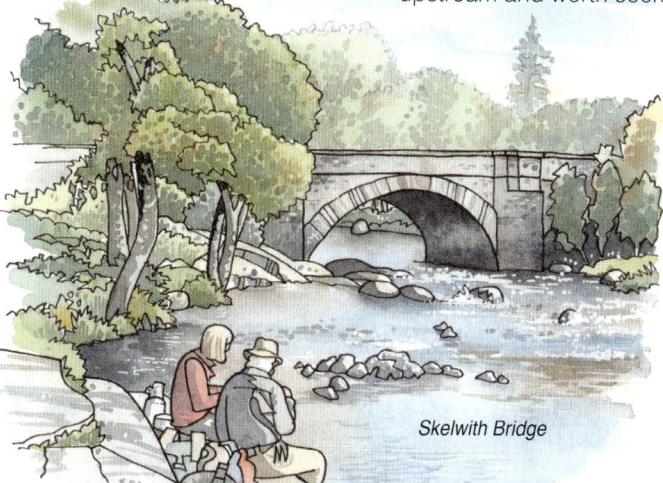

Chesters by the River

Skelwith Bridge

4 The Langdales

Ambleside

A bustling town of shops, hotels, guest houses, pubs and restaurants, superbly set between the head of Windermere and a panorama of shapely fells, Ambleside is the perfect base for exploring central Lakeland. There's everything the visitor needs – except maybe somewhere to park. Best to park on the outskirts and walk into town.

Ambleside has long been a popular stopping place for travellers. At the end of the 17th century it had five ale houses and a weekly market. Even though it only came as far as Windermere, the arrival of the railway in the mid-18th century opened up the area to a huge influx of visitors. Ambleside's first outdoor shop opened in 1959 and the number, and that of visitors, seems to have never stopped growing since.

Lake Road and High Pike

Market Place

Armitt Museum Acclaimed literary museum with more than 10,000 items on Lake District history and local personalities, including a lock of Ruskin's hair! A remarkable collection of Beatrix Potter's early studies of fungi and mosses demonstrate that artistically she was more than just an illustrator of fluffy bunnies.

Zeffirelli's Independant cinema with jazz bar and café.

St Mary's Church Built between 1850 and 1854 in Early Gothic style, designed by Sir George Gilbert Scott who was also responsible for London's Albert Memorial and St Pancras Station.

Galava The foundations of a Roman fort built to defend the road over HardKnott and Wrynose Passes to the port at Ravenglass.

Grasmere

Kirkstone Pass

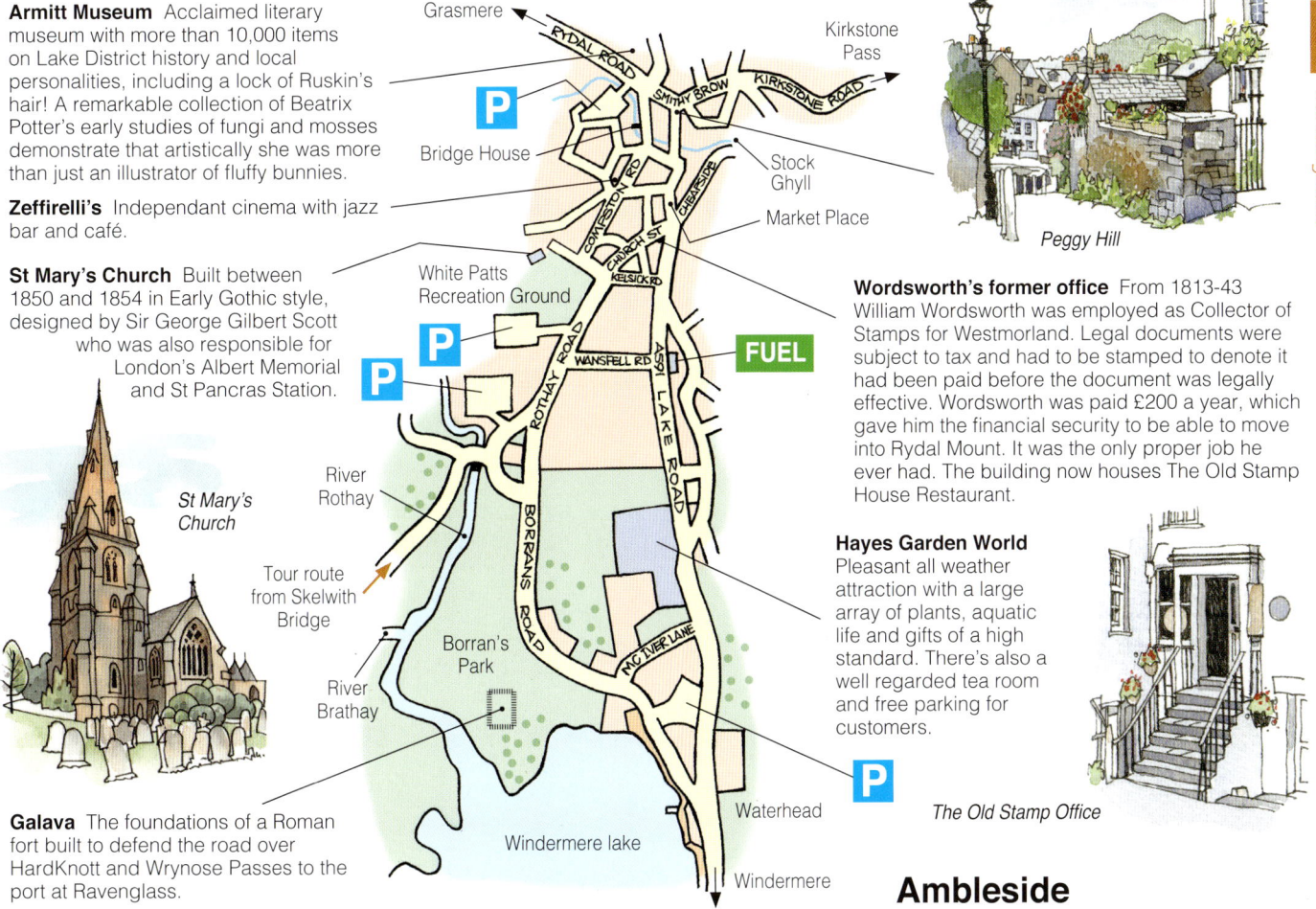

Bridge House

Stock Ghyll

Market Place

Peggy Hill

White Patts Recreation Ground

Wordsworth's former office From 1813-43 William Wordsworth was employed as Collector of Stamps for Westmorland. Legal documents were subject to tax and had to be stamped to denote it had been paid before the document was legally effective. Wordsworth was paid £200 a year, which gave him the financial security to be able to move into Rydal Mount. It was the only proper job he ever had. The building now houses The Old Stamp House Restaurant.

Hayes Garden World Pleasant all weather attraction with a large array of plants, aquatic life and gifts of a high standard. There's also a well regarded tea room and free parking for customers.

St Mary's Church

River Rothay

Tour route from Skelwith Bridge

River Brathay

Borran's Park

Waterhead

The Old Stamp Office

Windermere lake

Windermere

Ambleside

The Langdales

4

61

4

The Langdales

Bridge House

Ambleside was the focal point for the Victorian 'cocktail belt' which extended beween the town and Grasmere. A well-educated social and literary set, they did much for the area, not least founding the National Trust. Sadly their influence didn't extend to the local architecture and Ambleside still hasn't shaken off its air of Victorian grey slate dullness. There are bright spots, however, especially Stock Ghyll where the beck once drove five water mills. One, originally a bark crushing mill for making tannin used in the leather trade, has been converted to cottages and flats. Another, an old corn mill, boasts a replica overshot waterwheel. Stock Ghyll Force, a 70ft waterfall is a short walk upstream.

Ambleside's most iconic building, Bridge House, spans Stock Beck and has survived not only megastardom on calendars and postcards, and as a pottery ornament, but also the construction of Rothay Road in 1833.

Built as an apple store for nearby Ambleside Hall, it's now a rather cramped National Trust shop. The roof still has the original 17th-century 'wrestler' slates along the ridge. It's had many uses over the years, mainly for storage, but has served time as a weaver's workshop, a cobbler's and a tea room.

The converted tannin mill in Stock Ghyll

The best-looking part of Ambleside is the old village on Smithy Brow, the lower and steep slopes of Kirkstone Pass. There are some superb examples of 16th and 17th-century vernacular architecture, with characteristic huge chimneys, small windows and thick local stone walls.

Ash Tree Cottage

Windermere lake ends a mile short of Ambleside at Waterhead, which may come as a surprise to many day-trippers who leave the ferries from Bowness expecting to be in the town. In summer they can hire a horse-drawn carriage to transport them in style to the centre or take a minibus. A huddle of tourist shops do their best to cope with the Waterhead daytrippers, but the view across the lake, crowded with swans, ducks and boats, to a distant view of the Langdale Pikes, beats everything.

Waterhead

PIT STOPS

Ambleside is the premier gastro capital of all the Lake District towns. There's a huge range available, from fish and chips to fine dining, plus a host of cafés and pubs, so you need never go hungry or thirsty here. This is only a tiny selection of what the town has to offer:

Zeffirelli's
Funky modern restaurant in Compston Street. An Ambleside favourite, famous for its pizzas and a generally Italian vegetarian menu. The in-house cinema shows mainstream releases and indie, arthouse fare. Jazz bar upstairs with live music. Daytime café for coffee, cake etc. on the terrace. *zeffirellis.com*

Old Stamp House Restaurant
Fine dining in the cellars of a quirky historic building. Multi award-winning food, locally sourced meat and fish plus foraged ingredients from the Cumbrian hills and forests. *oldstamphouse.com*

Fellini's
The Church Street branch of the Zeffirelli family. Serves delicious vegetarian food inspired by the Mediterranean. Cinema shows live satellite performances from the world of opera, ballet and theatre, as well as arthouse and niche films. *fellinisambleside.com*

TOUR 5

Rheged to Ambleside • 30 miles

Rheged – Dalemain – Pooley Bridge – Ullswater – Aira Force – Glenridding – Patterdale – Hartsop – Brotherswater – Kirkstone Pass – Troutbeck – Ambleside

Starting at Rheged, modelled on a motorway service station but built in a disused lakeland quarry with leisure centre add-ons, this route continues to Dalemain, the area's major stately home. We visit Pooley Bridge, Ullswater's main tourist centre, recovering well from Storm Desmond devastation in 2015. A picturesque drive along the western lakeside side of Ullswater follows, taking in Aira Force, a pretty and popular waterfall. Glenridding and Patterdale are busy hiker villages, while peaceful Patterdale valley is almost surrounded by craggy fells. Kirkstone Pass, most famous and highest of the Lakeland passes, climbs over to Troutbeck, Beatrix Potter's favourite village and a mecca for lovers of vernacular architecture. The tour ends with a stately drive along the Windermere lakeside to Ambleside.

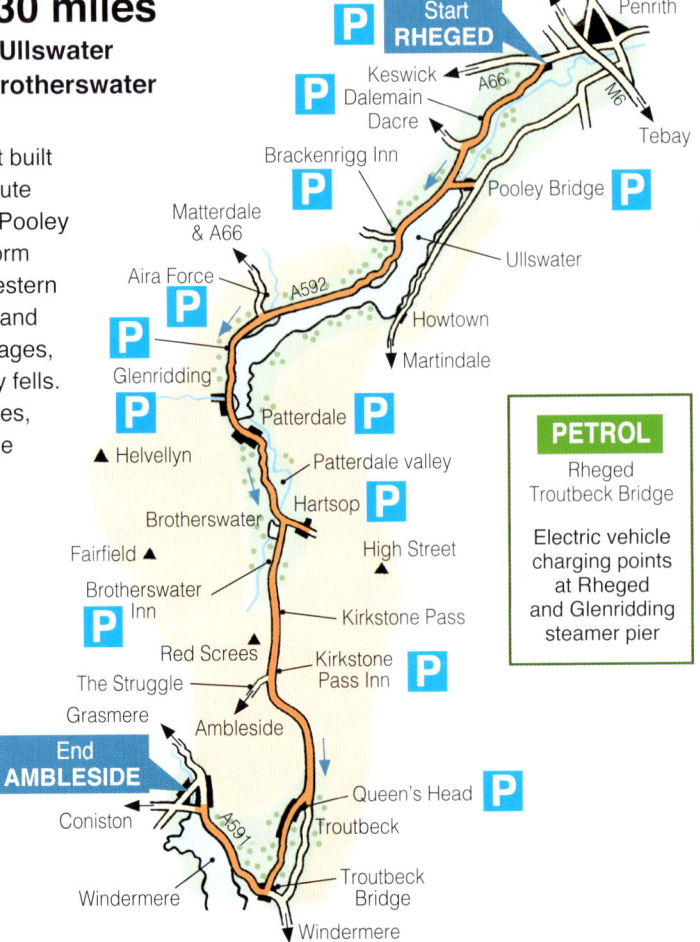

Troutbeck

Start RHEGED

End AMBLESIDE

PETROL

Rheged
Troutbeck Bridge

Electric vehicle charging points at Rheged and Glenridding steamer pier

64

The Tour

Join the A66 roundabout from Rheged and take the first exit on your left, the A592 signed Ullswater & Stainton. Proceed through open countryside with views to the distant Pennine hills. After a mile or so you join the River Eamont, outflow of Ullswater, and Dalemain country house set in its estate meadows.

Follow the broad Eamont for a while and Dunmallet, a pyramid-shaped hill covered in trees, comes into view ahead. A mile or so further on brings you to a T-junction with the B5230 on the shores of Ullswater. Turn left onto the lakeside road to Pooley Bridge. There's a car park beside the new bridge or you can cross it and try you luck at parking in the usually busy village.

Dalemain

ATTRACTIONS

Rheged

Built in a disused quarry, Rheged was opened in 2000, owned and run by the Dunning family who also own the Tebay Services Hotel on the M6 and the Gloucester services on the M5. It's Britain's largest grass-covered building and the biggest visitor attraction in Cumbria. The centre boasts a six-storey 3D cinema screen featuring a dramatic journey back in time through 2,000 years of Cumbria's history and mystery, as well as screenings of selected block-buster films. With a huge range of activities to keep all the family entertained, Rheged also hosts numerous exhibitions in a purpose-built area, regularly changing throughout the year. There's also shops, places to eat and a service station for motorists with fuel and charging for electric vehicles. rheged.com

Rheged

Dalemain

A large, Georgian-fronted house facing the A592, Dalemain developed from a peel tower built on the site during the reign of Henry II. Its Old Hall dates back to the 12th century, with wings added in the 16th century. The Hasell family have lived in the house since since 1679, when it was acquired by Sir Edward Hasell, steward to Lady Anne Clifford. The main frontage of fine pink sandstone was added in 1744. A labyrinth of unexpected spaces throughout the interior accommodate collections of fine furniture, portraits, ceramic dolls houses and toys.

The house benefits from five acres of spectacular gardens, which received the Garden of the Year Award in 2013. Plants include a Greek fir, which had been a gift from Joseph Banks, the botanist, in the 1840s.

In 2005, Dalemain founded and continues to host the World's Original Marmalade Awards & Festival, held in March each year, which has become an international landmark culinary event. There are plant sales, a tea shop in a baronial hall and a programme of events throughout the year. dalemain.com

Pooley Bridge

Sometimes unkindly branded a 'mini Bowness', Pooley Bridge is a small and busy little village situated at the north end of Ullswater. There's a general store, numerous gift shops, three pubs and a discrete gin shop, so tourists are well catered for.

For many years Pooley's most distinguishing feature was the narrow 18th-century bridge across the River Eamont, the outflow of Ullswater, and until the 1974 county reorganisation, the border between Cumberland and Westmorland.

Then Storm Desmond struck in December 2015, bringing unprecedented rainfall of almost 10 inches in 24 hours. Ullswater overflowed, luxury riverside houses were destroyed and the much-loved old bridge collapsed after flood water rose to the top of its walls.

The village was cut off from the west bank for four months until a temporary bridge was erected. A new steel construction was opened in October 2020.

Pooley Bridge (1764-2015)

Pooley Bridge Inn

A distinctive building, currently the '*Pooley Bridge Inn*' and formally the '*Chalet*', has overlooked the square for many years, looking as though it's a lost visitor to the Lake District from a *Heidi* Alpine tale.

The new Pooley Bridge (2020)

The brick-built Millennium Cross, erected in 2000 on the square outside the Crown Hotel, is topped by a shining metal fish weather vane. It commemorates the granting of a charter for a fish market from King John in the 12th century. At that time fishing was Pooley Bridge's main industry, with fish being caught from a pool (hence the village name) below the bridge, formed by damming the river. An earlier cross that stood here was removed in 1860 to make space for turning carriages. The latest cross now annoys motorists trying to park.

Dunmallet, the prominent tree-covered hill on the west bank of the Eamont, rises to 775ft. In his *Outlying Fells of Lakeland*, Wainwright describes the ascent from the riverside car park as a 'simple after-dinner stroll'.

Crown Hotel and the Millennium Cross

Granny Dowbekin's Tearoom

1863 Bistro

Sun Inn and Dunmallet

PIT STOPS

Crown Hotel
This refurbished 17th-century coaching inn with 17 guest bedrooms serves fairly standard gastropub fare, but the setting is sensational, with a large terrace going down to the riverside providing unrivalled views of Ullswater and the new bridge.
crownpooleybridge.co.uk

Sun Inn
Pooley's nearest thing to a village pub, converted from a row of cottages in the 1700s. Now family run with a carved panelled bar and a sunny beer garden. Nine *en-suite* rooms.
suninnpooleybridge.co.uk.

Granny Dowbekin's Tearoom
Well-regarded tearoom with a riverside terrace next to the bridge. Serves all-day breakfasts, main meals and home-made cakes to the recipes of the owner's great-great Lancastrian granny. Muddy boots and dogs welcome.
grannydowbekins.co.uk.

1863 Bistro
Situated at the quieter, eastern end of the village, this classy family-run bistro with rooms has garnered many foodie awards since opening in 2016. The building was originally a blacksmith's shop, built in 1863, and more recently the village post office.
1863ullswater.co.uk

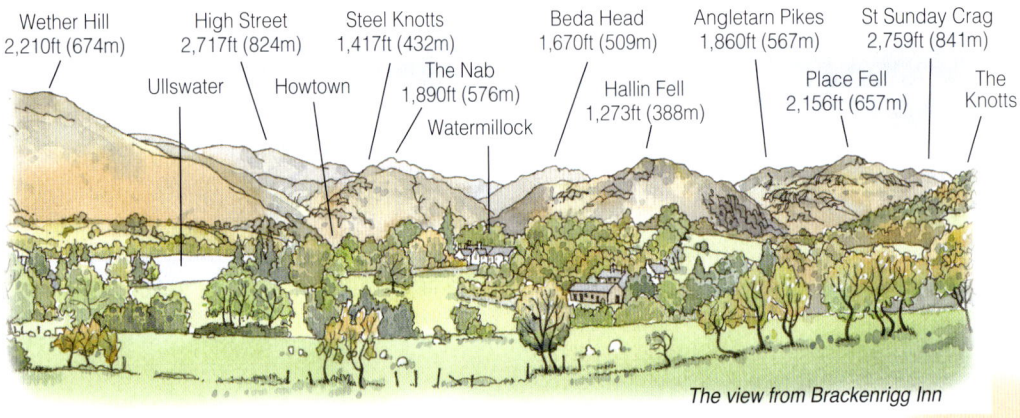

5 Rheged to Ambleside

The view from Brackenrigg Inn

Labels on view: Wether Hill 2,210ft (674m); High Street 2,717ft (824m); Steel Knotts 1,417ft (432m); Beda Head 1,670ft (509m); Angletarn Pikes 1,860ft (567m); St Sunday Crag 2,759ft (841m); Ullswater; Howtown; The Nab 1,890ft (576m); Hallin Fell 1,273ft (388m); Place Fell 2,156ft (657m); The Knotts; Watermillock

Map labels: River Eamont; Penrith; Dalemain; Pooley Bridge; Brackenrigg Inn; 'Steamer' route; Watermillock; Howtown; A66; Aira Force; Park Brow; Hallin Fell; Martindale; Birk Fell; Place Fell; Popular family walk; Slopes of Helvellyn; Glenridding; Patterdale; Kirkstone Pass

Leave Pooley Bridge and rejoin the A592 for a picturesque drive along the lakeside. Moving away from the lake, the road climbs to the Brackenrigg Inn, from where there's a terrific view across the lake to Howtown on the eastern shore. Continuing through meadows and hills you reach Aira Force, around five miles from Pooley Bridge. The A5091 climbs up Park Brow and eventually joins the A66 at Troutbeck, some five miles away.

Ullswater

For many people the finest of all the lakes, Ullswater has the shape of an elongated 'Z' with three distinct reaches. There's the gentle, almost boring, landscape at the northern, Pooley Bridge end, the more scenic central section and the full on grandeur and mountain magnificence of the southern part at Glenridding.

Ullswater snakes its way through the landscape for around seven and a half miles. It's almost a mile wide and 205 feet deep, with five small islands, all at the southern end. The famous steamers call at four piers around the lake.

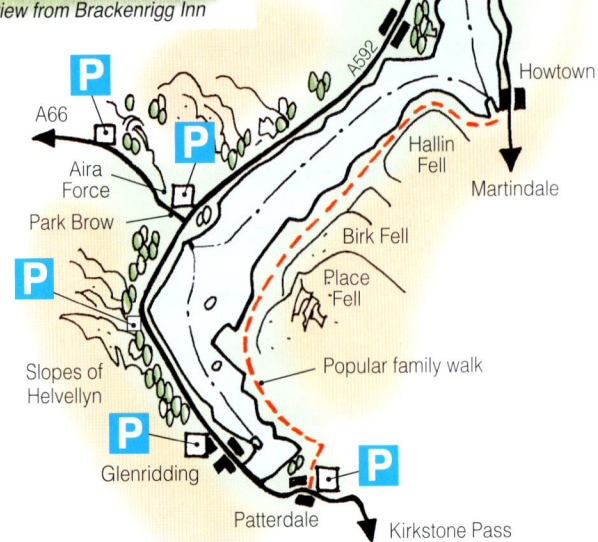

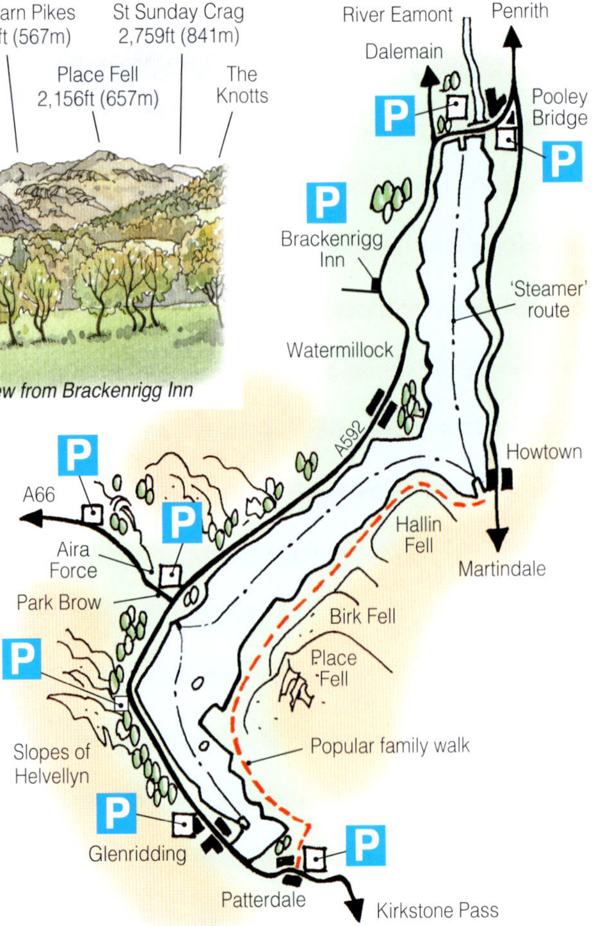

One of the most popular family walks in the Lake District is to take the steamer from Glenridding to Howtown, then walk back along an idyllic footpath of mixed woodland and rocky crags along the eastern lakeshore. Unlike many of the other large lakes, Ullswater has few lakeside paths and it's difficult to walk off-road around it, which makes the Howtown to Glenridding route even more special.

In the early 1960's a plan to turn the lake into a reservoir, increasing the level of the lake by three feet, was defeated after a furious outcry led by Norman Lord Birkett in the House of Lords, resulting in the proposal being thrown out. His crusade is commemorated with a plaque near the steamer pier at Pooley Bridge and the naming of Birkett Fell overlooking the lake.

Brackenrigg Inn

Aira Force
ATTRACTION

A mile before entering Ullswater, gentle Aira Beck turns into a wild waterfall, Aira Force, plunging 65 feet into a picturesque 'fairy dell' much beloved by Victorian tourists and many more since. A small arched bridge spans the stream above the waterfall and provides a spectacular viewpoint as the water gathers speed for its leap. Another bridge at the bottom allows you to get close to the action.

Aira Force provides full tourist facilities, including parking and graded walks. It's an excellent place to just wander through the woods or relax with a coffee and tasty treat in the tearoom.
nationaltrust.org.uk/aira-force

Brackenrigg Inn
PIT STOP

This former 18th-century coaching inn prides itself on serving traditional, home cooked, Cumbrian cuisine, using some of the finest locally-sourced ingredients. Its own microbrewery produces five brands of real ale and there's a wide range of *en-suite* accommodation, some with a wonderful view across Ullswater.
brackenrigginn.co.uk

Aira Force

5

Rheged to Ambleside

The view of the southern reach of Ullswater from Park Brow, on the Matterdale road near Aira Force, is justifiably famous and not just for its outstanding scenic qualities.

On this stretch of water in 1955 Donald Campbell set the world waterspeed record, when he piloted the jet-propelled hydroplane Bluebird K7 to a speed of 202.32mph.

The lakeside below Aira Force is also where in 1802 William Wordsworth and his sister Dorothy are reputed to have seen the daffodils that inspired William's most famous piece of poetry. The couple were going home after staying at Eusemere, a country house at Pooley Bridge, the home of the anti-slavery campaigner Thomas Clarkson.

They were walking to Grasmere, some 15 miles away as the crow flies, which could have included a 2000ft climb on the old pack horse road over Grisedale Hause. They may also have been carrying luggage and wearing ordinary clothes, rather than hundreds of pounds worth of gear from an Ambleside outdoor shop.

The popular caricature of the wimpy Lakeland Romantic Poets is blown away by their prodigous walks. Robert Southy is said to have regularly visited the Wordsworths, walking from Keswick to Grasmere, taking in Helvellyn on the way. William and Dorothy were phenomenal walkers. De Quincey, in his *Recollection of the Lake Poets*, famously calculates that Wordsworth's legs 'must have traversed a distance of 175 to 180,000 English miles'.

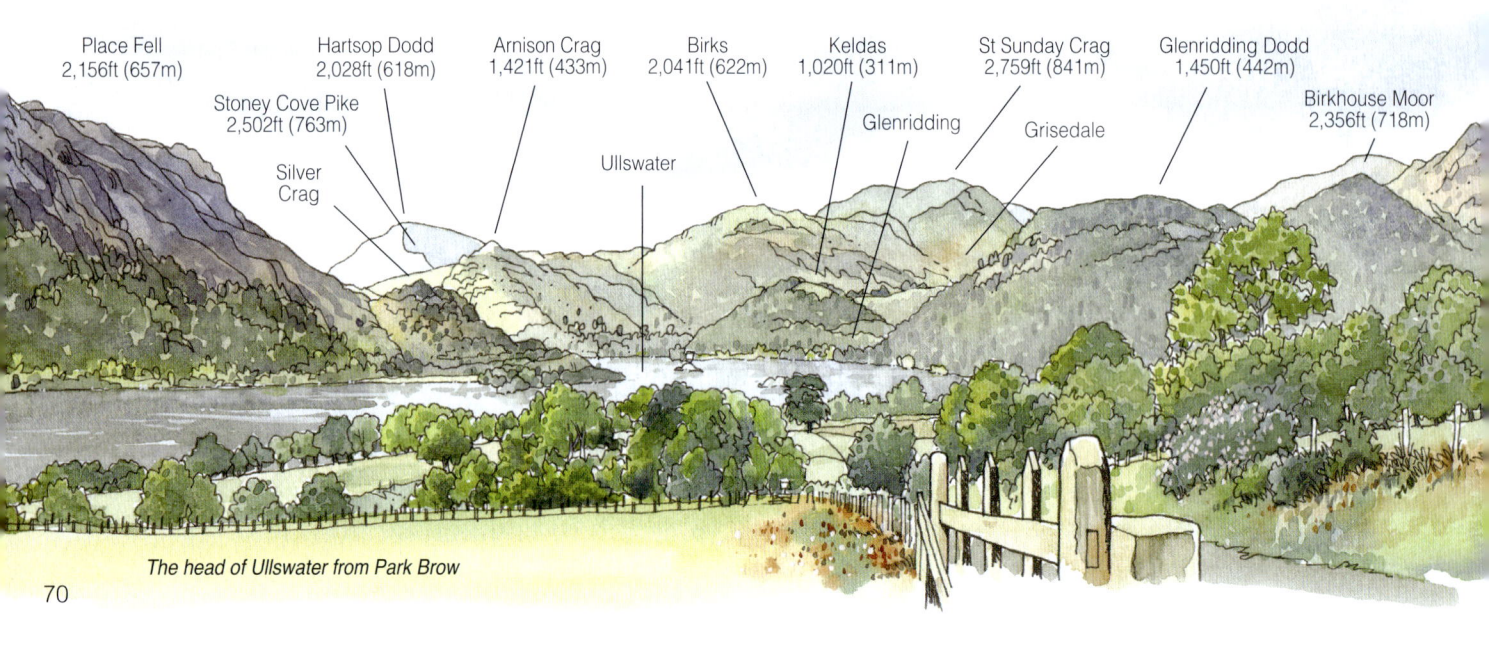

The head of Ullswater from Park Brow

From Aira Force the lakeside road swings left around Gowbarrow Bay into the third section of the lake where the big mountains are gathered. The car park here is a good place to stop for a while and take in the magnificent surroundings. The route continues through woodland, twisting and turning around rocky outcrops before reaching Glenridding. The village was isolated at the head of the lake for many years until part of Gowbarrow Crag was blasted away in the 1920s to make room for the new metalled road. Glenridding has a huge car park and there's plenty to see.

Glenridding

Once one of the country's most prosperous mining areas, Glenridding now caters for the thousands of visitors who make the village their base for climbing some of Lakeland's finest fells, particulary Helvellyn by its most challenging route along Striding Edge.

The village itself is little more than a couple of rows of former miner's cottages set back from the lake, a general store, numerous tearooms and B&Bs, plus a couple of upmarket hotels. There's also a pleasant park by the steamer pier.

Gold and silver were found here in the 19th century, but the Greenside mine at the head of Glenridding Beck was exceptionally rich in lead. The mines were worked out by 1962 after a record 300 years of continuous production. The last level ran for 3,000 feet into the Helvellyn range.

Glenridding Beck runs through the village and over the years has caused it much grief. A dam, built high in the hills to provide power for the mines, burst at Kepple Cove in 1927, causing tons of water and rubble to sweep down the beck into the lake, bringing devastation to the village on its way. There has been periods of serious flooding since, with Storm Desmond bringing unprecedented destruction in 2015.

Slopes of Birkhouse Moor

Sheffield Pike 2,214ft (675m)

Slopes of Glenridding Dodd

Stybarrow Dodd 2,766ft (843m)

Traveller's Rest. Once the first port of call for thirsty miners after a shift

Glenridding from the lakeside

5 Ullswater 'Steamers'

The 'steamers' are a popular Ullswater attraction providing regular trips up and down the lake, calling at Pooley Bridge, Howtown, Aira force and Glenridding 363 days a year. From the 1850s they were working boats, moving mail, workers and goods to and from the Greenside lead mine at Glenridding.

Today there are five heritage vessels – now diesel powered – plying the tourist trade. *Raven* and *Lady of the Lake* were converted from steam in the 1930s.

'Lady of the Lake'

Lady of the Lake was launched on 26th June 1877 and is believed to be the oldest working passenger vessel in the world.

Raven, launched on the 11th July 1889, was directly inspired and suggested by the tour operator Thomas Cook.

Western Belle was built in 1935. After working on the Rivers Tamar, Yealm and Thames, she was refurbished and launched on Ullswater in 2011.

Lady Dorothy, originally a sea going vessel from Guernsey, joined the fleet in 2001.

Lady Wakefield was built in 1949, fully restored and renamed by HRH Princess Alexandra in 2007.

Glenridding Pier House has two free-to-use electric car charging points.

'Raven' at the Glenridding pier

PIT STOPS

Glenridding has a lot to offer for quick bites, with tables and chairs seemingly set up wherever there's an open space. Here are a few suggestions:

Fellbites
Next to the car park, this is a cheery café by day and a restaurant by night. Hiker-friendly, with breakfasts, burgers and sandwiches. There's pub-style grub in the evening *fellbitescafe.co.uk*

Helvellyn Country Kitchen
Located alongside the beck, this family-run café provides good home-cooked food freshly prepared on the premises from locally sourced ingredients. They also bake their own bread and bagettes. Breakfast, Lunch, Dinner, and Brunch. Outside seating. Takeaway facility. Big range of teas and coffees. *helvellyncountrykitchen.co.uk*

Travellers Rest
Popular village pub on the hillside above the village. Fairly standard pub food with outdoor seating and fabulous views across the village to the lake.

For more upmarket dining try one of the two main hotels in the village.
theglenriddinghotel.com
lakedistricthotels.net/innonthelake

Continue on the A592 to the head of Ullswater and Patterdale village. More twists in the road takes you into Patterdale itself, a lovely valley edged by craggy hills. Goldrill Beck, which flows through the dale is prone to floods and the substantial bridges north of the Brotherswater outflow are built to cope.

Hartsop, a small and ancient hamlet, lies just off the main road and is well worth a visit for anyone interested in vernacular architecture. There's a small car park at the eastern end, but apart from the wonderful buildings the settlement has no facilities for visitors.

The White Lion bottleneck

Patterdale

A widely scattered village almost seamlessly joined to Glenridding, Patterdale is prettier than it's neighbour and feels more like a real village. Both settlements are hugely popular for their location, attracting multitudes of boot-shod visitors year round, though those at Patterdale are a more sedate variety rather than the adrenalin-fuelled adventurers at Glenridding setting out to conquer Helvellyn. Patterdale retains a slightly old-fashioned air and still has a busy village store and post office. The wedge-shaped White Lion Inn, set at a bottleneck in the main road, is a popular (though not with motorists!) landmark.

Patterdale village

White Lion Inn — PIT STOP

Generally regarded to be the best pub in the area, the White Lion is dog and vegetarian friendly, and serves 'the most delicious food and the finest drinks, including a good choice of Real Ales'. There are seven rooms to let, five *en suite*. Generous breakfasts are served until 4pm! A popular folk tale has it that Wordsworth was at the White Lion bar as news arrived that Nelson had died at Trafalgar. *whitelionpatterdale.com*

Patterdale

A favourite Lakeland valley for many people, (including a certain A Wainwright), Patterdale stretches for three glorious miles from Kirkstone Pass to Ullswater. A narrow band of farmland twists through an avenue of fells, while Goldrill Beck flows attractively out of Brotherswater and the A592 road winds through mixed woodland and pasture. There's a scattering of picturesque farms, and houses laden with flowers in summer,

As the only direct route between Ullswater and Windermere, it's usually busy with traffic all year, but there's a quiet walking track from Hartsop to Patterdale along the eastern side of the valley with fine views of the dale, Ullswater and the Helvellyn range of fells.

View south from mid-Patterdale

Deepdale

Three delightful smaller dales go off to the west of the main valley. Grisedale rises from the village of Patterdale to Grisedale Hause, climbing between Fairfield and Seat Sandal, then down to Grasmere. Deepdale and Dovedale cut deep into the fells and both have superb arrangements of crags at their head. There's a terrific view of Dovedale from further along this tour.

Patterdale is prone to flooding after heavy rain and was particularly badly hit by a huge downpour in November 2009 and Storm Desmond in 2015.

Hartsop

A delightful hamlet, snuggled between steep fells in a cul-de-sac at the southern end of Patterdale, Hartsop was once the biggest settlement and centre of industry in the valley. Renowned for wool spinning, it also had corn and cloth mills with tailors, cobblers and blacksmiths looking after the needs of the locally-based miners.

These days the 17th-century, grey-stone cottages are quiet, their spinning galleries prettified with potted plants; only the sounds of sheep, the tinkling of Pasture Beck and the occasional yap of a farm dog disturbs the refined air.

The 17th-century Low House Farm on the approach to the village is a splendid example of a vernacular architecture Lakeland farmstead, where a barn and cattle shed were built at opposite ends of the house to keep the humans warm. Fell Yeat was once the Bunch o' Birks Inn on a pack horse trail that still crosses the beck at a ford, before winding its sinuous way to Kirkstone Pass.

Apart from a rough car park at the far end of the village, where a wide track sweeps up the valley to Hayeswater, there are no facilities. But with a place as picturesque as Hartsop, 'facilities' would only be a vulgar intrusion.

Low House Farm

Cottage with a stepped spinning gallery

5 *Continue on the A592 to Brotherswater, an odd-shaped lake with a slightly brooding atmosphere. The Brotherswater Inn, just south of the lake, is a good place to stop and take in the fabulous mountain scenery before tackling the famous Kirkstone Pass.*

A stop at the inn on the summit is mandatory, not only for its excellent sustenance but also to take in the sensational views and the bracing fresh air.

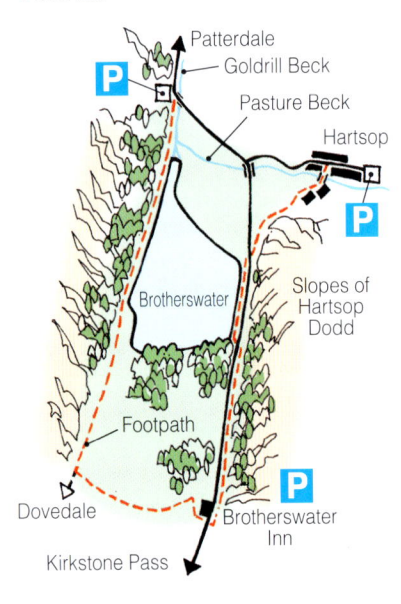

Middle Dodd 2,146ft (657m)
High Hartsop Dodd 1,703ft (519m)
Dovedale
Caiston Gill

Brotherswater Inn and the approach to Kirkstone Pass

Brotherswater

A curious, almost square-shaped lake, Brotherswater is around 560 yards long and 440 yards wide, entirely filling the valley floor and giving it the look of a flooded field. Underground springs on the bed cause the thickness of ice on the surface to vary, which may account for two brothers being drowned while skating sometime during the 18th century and prompting the lake's name change from the original Broadwater.

Whether Brotherswater is actually a 'lake' can be a subject for hot debate and it's often omitted from the classic list of sixteen lakes as being only a 'tarn'. It's a issue that seems to go in and out of fashion and will probably never be decisively resolved.

Kirkstone Pass

Historically a drovers' track, Kirkstone Pass connects Patterdale to Windermere and Ambleside. At 1,489ft, it's the highest motor pass in the Lake District. The Patterdale side is steep (25% in places) but the road is fairly broad and sweeping.

The climb out of Ambleside is particularly steep with some awkward corners needing careful attention, even in a modern car. The final stretch is called 'The Struggle' because 19th-century travellers had to get out of their coaches and walk alongside their weary horses up to the inn. You only have to look at it to see why.

The pass is named after the large standing stone, shaped like a kirk (church), on the Patterdale side, near the summit.

Kirkstone Pass from Patterdale

The Kirkstone Pass Inn

The Kirkstone Pass Inn stands at the summit of the pass and was once an important coaching stop. Now catering primarily for tourists, it enjoys the highest location of any public house in Cumbria and the third highest in England. Dating back to 1496, the building had the tall part added in the early 1800s as a coach house high enough to accomodate the carriages of the day. Around the 1950's it became a garage with petrol pumps and has now been converted into a cottage. Creditably green, the inn's water comes off the fell behind the building and a revolutionary wind turbine and battery system generates all its electricity.

PIT STOPS

Brotherswater Inn
Serves Full English breakfast and has a filling traditional bar menu, including Cumberland sausages, braised lamb and homemade pies. There's also seven B&B rooms, all with a sensational mountain backdrop. *sykeside.co.uk*

Kirkstone Pass Inn
Five-star hygiene rated food, accomodation and real ales. Hearty homemade local dishes, with a selection of veggie meals and an open log fire when it's cold. Staying guests can enjoy a four-poster suite with shower room or a choice of *en-suite* B&Bs. There's also a budget bothy that sleeps 12 (bring your own sleeping bag) with central heating and a hot shower. *kirkstonepassinn.com*

5 Rheged to Ambleside

The A592 continues down the south side of the pass, twisting through barren moorland to an airy hillside where there's a drop of some 200 feet over the roadside wall to Troutbeck Park Farm, once owned by Beatrix Potter, in the valley below. At a Y-junction, take the rising road on your right, signed Ambleside. The Queen's Head Hotel stands on the A592 at the junction and the Mortal Man inn is 500 yards further along the village road. Parking is difficult, with the Institute and tearoom at the village centre the best place to stop. Townend, a historic 17th-century house, stands at a Y-junction at the the southern end. Take the left hand arm, signed Windermere, which leads to the A591 at Troutbeck Bridge where there's a handy petrol station just across the road. Turn right here, signed Ambleside & Keswick, for a lovely seven-mile drive along the northern end of Windermere to Ambleside and the end of this tour.

Troutbeck

The Institute and Old Post Office Tearoom

Clinging to the hillside of a long, green valley, Troutbeck consists of a series of picturesque hamlets strung for more than a mile along an old pack-horse road, from Ambleside to Kentmere, linked by a network of footpaths and lanes. Many of the houses are of 17th-century origin and some still have spinning galleries and mullioned windows. The modern A592 road bypasses the village, leaving it in peace for walkers and lovers of vernacular architecture, for whom Troutbeck is endlessly fascinating.

The curiously-named Jownie Wife House

PIT STOP
Old Post Office Tearoom
A traditional village shop selling all the essentials. Also serves tea, coffee and cold drinks with homemade soups, fresh scones etc, and the best ever Kendal flapjacks. *troutbeck.org*

Queen's Head Hotel on the A592 road

Townend
ATTRACTION

Built in 1626 for George Browne, a wealthy yeoman farmer, Townend remained in the hands of eleven generations of the same family for over 300 years until 1943, when the National Trust took it over. Most of the contents remain intact, a remarkable record of one prosperous Lakeland family's history.

The building was extensively restored in 2016 and in a village of architectural gems Townend, with its bulky round chimneys so beloved by Wordsworth, reigns supreme. There's a colourful cottage-style garden outside and across the road a magnificent bank barn where the Browne's used to store wool fleeces before being sold to merchants. *nationaltrust.org.uk/townend*

Townend

Queen's Head
PIT STOPS

Reopened in April 2017 after a £2 million refurbishment, the new Queen's Head features cosy drinking and dining areas with 10 comfortable en-suite guest bedrooms. Dog and vegan friendly. A new menu highlights a mix of homely classic pub food with Cumbrian flair. *robinsonsbrewery/queensheadtroutbeck*

Mortal Man
With a history going back to 1689 this is a quirky traditional English Inn boasting 12 letting rooms, a great atmosphere, a well stocked bar, roaring fires, delicious food and possibly the best beer garden in the UK. *themortalman.co.uk*

Mortal Man

The Bank Barn

Beatrix Potter bought Troutbeck Park Farm, a run down 1,900-acre sheep farm at the head of the valley in 1923. With Tom Storey, her faithful shepherd, she built up a celebrated flock of Herdwick sheep and began her life-long mission to save old farm estates from developers. She said Troutbeck valley was her favourite place. It's easy to see why. Her muse is all around.

TOUR 6

Keswick, Back o' Skiddaw & Caldbeck Round • 33 miles

Keswick – Uldale – Back o' Skiddaw – Caldbeck – Hesket Newmarket – Mungrisdale – Threlkeld – Keswick

PETROL — Keswick, Caldbeck

Bassenthwaite & Skiddaw

From Keswick we head north through the woodland beneath Skiddaw, with an opportunity to visit Mirehouse, a major stately home. Continuing past Bassenthwaite Lake, the route climbs steadily into the wild country Back o' Skiddaw. Uldale is a welcoming farming village, from where we cross open moorland to the delightful village of Caldbeck.

Beyond pretty Hesket Newmarket we're back into wild country, with great fell views, before reaching Mungrisdale and joining the A66. The hamlet of Scales clings to the lower slopes of Blencathra and motorists can enjoy close up views of the mountain's soaring ridges. After a visit to Threlkeld the tour ends where it began at Keswick

The Tour

Leave Keswick, turning right near the petrol station at High Hill, signed Penrith. Pass the Pheasant Inn and cross the A66 at the roundabout onto the A591, signed Carlisle. After around three miles you reach the southern end of Bassenthwaite and enter Dodd Wood. The Old Sawmill Tearoom is on your right with a car park for Mirehouse.

A half mile or so further on there's a narrow lane on your left, signed Bassenthwaite Church ¾, a diversion to St Begas Church on the shore of Bassenthwaite Lake (details in Tour 3, page 48).

The road then twists and turns through farmland to the Castle Inn crossroads, where you should turn right onto a minor road signed Caldbeck 8. After a steady climb of around three miles, with great fell views, you enter the small village of Uldale.

Mirehouse

Built in 1666 by the Earl of Derby, Mirehouse is the epitome of the English country manor house. Since 1802 it has been the home of the Spedding family, who are often on hand to show visitors around. A pianist plays in the music room. James Spedding, a noted 19th-century literary figure, became friends with Tennyson and Thackeray while they were at Cambridge University. During one of his visits to Mirehouse Tennyson was working on his epic poem *Morte d'Arthur,* and it's said that he used Bassenthwaite as the setting for Arthur's death. James Spedding spent most of his life writing a 14-volume biography of Francis Bacon. His father, John, also had literary connections, having spent six years as a classmate of William Wordsworth at Hawkshead Grammar School. Some of Wordsworth's letters can be seen in the house. Over the years it has been adapted for several households to live in, but much of the house is still open to the public.

Mirehouse

Old Sawmill Tearoom

Mirehouse
A major literary home with a welcome for families and children. Interesting collection of eclectic period items. Nature trail and an adventure playground in the grounds with Bassenthwaite Lake's only east-shore walk. As a family home, opening times are restricted. Check before visiting. *mirehouse.co.uk*

ATTRACTION & PIT STOP

Old Sawmill Tearoom
Specialises in homemade Cumbrian cooking. Cakes, scones, sandwiches, soups and hot dishes, all made on the premises. Dogs welcome at the tables outside the café.

6 Uldale

Uldale is a typical north lakes village attractively built on hillsides at the edge of the National Park. There are a few farms, old cottages converted to desirable residences and B&Bs, plus a popular pub, The Snooty Fox, catering for local and passing tourist trade.

A Norse-Irish settlement existed here in the 9th-century with the name Uldale coming from Norse meaning 'wolf'. Dale wolves once roamed the fells around here in abundance. A sheep farming area since medieval times, in 1791 a sheep fair was established in the village. Abandoned copper and limestone quarries – and the existence of a pub – are evidence of 19th-century mining in the area between the village and Caldbeck.

Uldale was the setting of David's House in Sir Hugh Walpole's *Herries Chronicles*. Indeed, much of the village and its surroundings feature in two other novels, *Judith Paris* and *The Fortress*. Huntsman John Peel spent the latter part of his life here after marrying an Uldale girl, Mary White.

Uldale

The Caldbeck and Uldale fells to the south are generally dull and featureless, apart from a few farms and the occasional walkers and cyclists. Yet there's a lot to be said for solitude. Back o' Skiddaw can be the perfect antidote to some over-crowded parts of the area.

The actual Back o' Skiddaw (or to be strictly accurate, the 'side' of Skiddaw) is a fine sight from the Uldale area. The long ridge of Long Side and Ullock Pike curves dramatically down to Bassenthwaite and the 'secret' valleys of Barkbethdale and Southerndale are revealed.

There are many surprises around here but probably none as stark as Over Water, a small lake set amongst fields along a back road from Uldale. A reservoir for the town of Wigton, it was created by a dam in the 1920s. It's now owned by the National Trust, but strictly private.

The Snooty Fox

Over Water

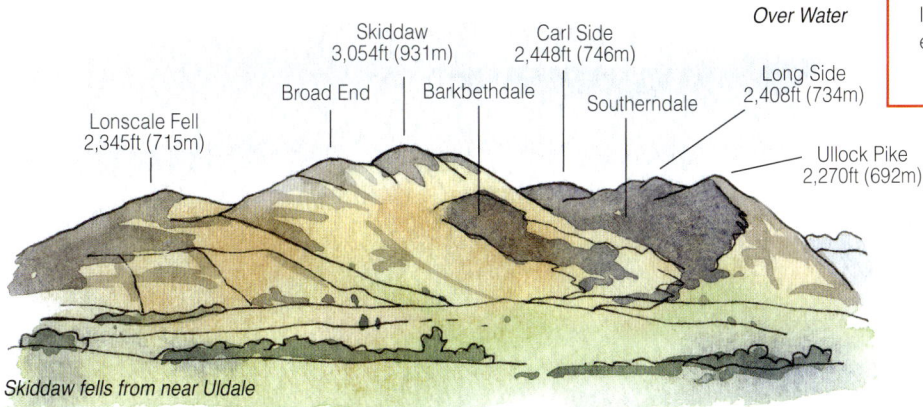

PIT STOPS

Snooty Fox
The hub of the local community, this friendly pub dates back to 1624 and offers a wide selection of locally brewed cask-conditioned ales, fine wines and malt whiskies, complimented by home-cooked food using the finest, locally-sourced, seasonal ingredients.

There are two cosy bars and a restaurant, plus two *en-suite* guest bedrooms. Note: the Snooty Fox is closed at lunchtimes.
snootyfoxuldale.co.uk

Mae's Tearoom
Situated in Uldale's Old School building (dated 1895), Mae's is a unique family-run tearoom and gallery offering teas, coffees and homemade traditional food. Evening meals on Fridays & Saturdays plus Sunday lunches, curry nights and live music. Open every day. *measctearooms.co.uk*

Lonscale Fell 2,345ft (715m)
Broad End
Skiddaw 3,054ft (931m)
Barkbethdale
Carl Side 2,448ft (746m)
Southerndale
Long Side 2,408ft (734m)
Ullock Pike 2,270ft (692m)

Skiddaw fells from near Uldale

Mae's Tearoom

6

Continue up the hill out of Uldale and look out for the view on your left across the Solway Firth to the Scottish hills. After you cross a cattle grid, the now unfenced road levels out onto broad moorland. A wonderful two miles follows as the switchback road crosses what has been described as one of the true wilderness areas of the Lake District where sheep, cattle (and sometimes cyclists and walkers) roam free.

Parkend marks a return to civilisation with a farm, requisite white cottages and a packhorse bridge over Parkend Beck. Another mile or so following the beck through pleasant farmland brings you to Caldbeck, one of North Lakeland's most attractive and interesting villages.

Former brewery and mill buildings

Caldbeck

Set in a limestone basin, hard up against the northern fells on the edge of the National Park, Caldbeck, now peaceful and residential, was once one of the Lake District's great mining centres.

It's most spectacular growth was in the 18th and 19th centuries, when 14 mines, mainly yielding silver, copper and lead, were sunk deep into the wild fells above the village. Caldbeck prospered with more than a dozen mills and a brewery along the River Caldew. Coal for local use was even mined within the village itself from shallow pits on Ratten Row, which fringes the village green. The population grew to 1,500 and with thirteen ale-houses it must have been a wild and woolly place. The last mine closed in 1965.

Standing near the bridge over the Calder at the southern end of the village green, the brewery and Lord's Mill are now desirable private houses. The brewery was formerly a wheat mill dating back to 1670. Brewing began in 1810 and ceased along with the industrial boom at the end of the 19th century. Lord's Mill, still with its checker-brick chimney, ground corn from 1704 to 1914.

Look out for a sign on a barn that directs you across fields to a ruined bobbin mill in 'The Howk'. Here the river has formed a spectacular gorge in the limestone with two deep holes where the water spins and froths with agitation. The romantic Victorians loved to gather here for picnics, with the local paper printing weather forecasts for them.

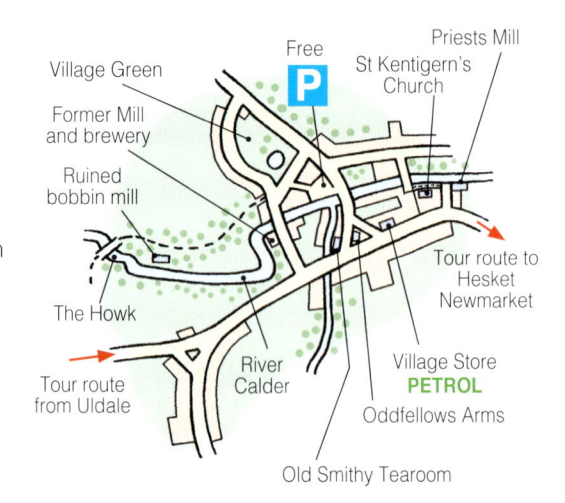

St Kentigern's Church

Cottages along the River Caldew

The 12th-century Church of St Kentigern catches the eye and attracts many visitors, many to visit the grave of John Peel, the Lakeland hunter of foxes immortalised in song. In 1829, a friend of Peel's, John Graves, wrote some words about him which, set to a popular Scottish folk tune, were sung in the local pub, The Oddfellows Arms. After tweaking by the choirmaster of Carlisle Cathedral, William Metcalf, *D'ye ken John Peel* was sung in London and the worldwide hit was born. Aged 78, Peel died of a hunting accident in 1854, with thousands of people turning out for his funeral. Mary Robinson, the Beauty of Buttermere, (see Tour 2) is also buried in the churchyard.

Former home of John Graves

The Oddfellows Arms on the village square

6

These days Caldbeck is largely residential and though visitors are well catered for, the village character hasn't been overwhelmed by tourism. Situated in the Tithe Barn next to the store, Hesta Scene is an alternative gift shop and gallery selling locally handmade items for the home. Well worth a visit.

The village layout makes it ideal for a circular walk. At the lovely stone bridge behind the church take the short pathway along the river to Priest Mill, built on the Caldew in 1701 by the rector. It's now converted into three craft workshops and has an excellent atmospheric tea room and restaurant, The Watermill Cafe.

woolclip.com
littlecrookedtree.co.uk
facebook.com/Caldbeck-Crafters-Co-op

Old Smithy Tearoom

Priest's Mill

PIT STOPS

Oddfellows Arms
Family-run village pub with ten well-appointed bedrooms. Cumbrian dishes prepared from local produce. Well-stocked bar with Jennings beers.
oddfellows-caldbeck.co.uk

Kirkland Store
Family-owned village shop and post office supplying all the essentials plus fresh rolls and pies, coffee and locally-made cakes. Petrol and diesel fuel is also available – the only filling station for several miles in the northern fells area.
caldbeckvillage.co.uk

Watermill Café
Situated on the upper floor of Priest's Mill overlooking the river and the village cricket field. Tea, coffee & light refreshments plus lunches. Friendly, cosy and great food. Highly recommended.
info@watermillcafe.co.uk
Tel: 016974-78267

Old Smithy Tearoom
Popular café-style tearoom with good reviews. Afternoon teas, home-baked cakes and scones. Hot meals and light lunches. Mooman's scrumptious homemade ice cream.
Tel: 016974-78378

Take the road out of Caldbeck past the church, heading for Hesket Newmarket, just over a mile away and another North Lakeland village gem.

Leave at the bottom end of the green, taking the road on the right past Denton House B&B. At a Y-junction take the right fork (Pasture Lane), signed Mungrisedale 6.

Hesket Newmarket

Closely bound with Caldbeck, Hesket Newmarket is another attractive village tucked into the Caldbeck fells. Its mainly 18th-century houses cluster around a five-acre traditional village green edged by a village shop/tearoom and a pub (The Old Crown) that serves its own beer brewed behind the building.

Hesket Hall, a prominent square house at the top end of the village, was built around 1630 for Sir Wilfrid Lawson, twice MP for Cockermouth. The shape of the house is all angles and annexes, said to be so that shadows from the twelve corners of the building would act as a sundial. The road haulage empire of Eddie Stobart began in this remote Lakeland hamlet.

The Old Crown

PIT STOPS

Hesket Newmarket Shop
The heart of the community with a post office and popular tearoom. Proud to offer the products of some 30 local suppliers including honey, pies, sausages and ready meals. *hesketnewmarketshop.co.uk*

The Old Crown
Britain's first co-operative pub bought by some 150 local residents in 2003. 'Regulars and visitors alike will always find a warm welcome, good home-cooked food, a friendly smile and a superb range of real ales.' The Hesket Newmarket Brewery behind the pub is also owned by a collective formed in 1995. Now a thriving microbrewery, it sells its famous beers such as *Skiddaw Special* and *Doris' 90th Birthday Ale* across a wide area. *theoldcrownpub.co.uk*

Hesket Newmarket

Dry stone walls edge the road as it narrows and the Blencathra massif begins to dominate the skyline ahead.

At a sharp left turn near some farm buildings, cross a cattle grid into open, unfenced moorland. An interesting couple of miles follows as Carrock Fell rears dramatically on your right and remnants of the ancient Greystoke Forest carpets the distant low hills on your left. Ahead rises the cone-shaped Mell Fell and the distant Ullswater fells.

Roadside dry stone walls return at Mosedale, a huddle of farm buildings at the foot of the Mosedale valley, which opens westwards to the Ullock and Caldbeck fells. A mile or so further on you enter the small village of Mungrisdale. The junction with the A66 is a couple of miles further on.

Traffic sweeps off Troutbeck Moor at speed, so you need to take extra care turning right onto the busy highway.

The A66 has many critics but the section from here to Keswick passes through some of the most dramatic and attractive scenery to be seen from any road in the Lake District.

Carrock Fell attracts many enthusiasts including geologists, mineralogists, archaeologists and rock climbers. The summit is ringed by the collapsed walls of an ancient hill-fort of unknown age and origin, but thought to be early English.

The Carrock Mine closed decades ago but the site can be reached at the end of a surfaced road from Mosedale, signed Swinside. It yielded a variety of minerals including wolfram, from which tungsten is made, the only source outside Cornwall. Carrock is also the only climbing-ground in the Northern Fells. The Eastern side is of Gabbro, an ideal rock for the sport, attracting local bouldering and slab climbing devotees.

The Caldew Valley & Carrock Fell

Souther Fell overlooks Mungrisdale and though of lowly altitude (1713ft/ 522m) it occupies an important position as the cornerstone of the Northern Fells.

The fell is also famous for its Spectral Army. On the afternoon of Midsummer Day 1745, a line of marching troops, cavalry and carriages was seen travelling along the summit ridge of Souther Fell. The procession continued for some hours until nightfall watched by 26 'sober and respected' witnesses who next day swore under oath to what they had seen. Sadly, the Spectral Army has never been seen since.

The infant River Glenderamackin almost encircles the base of Souther Fell like a moat, only becoming a 'real' river at the bridge at Mungrisdale. The small village has some attractive houses, a church on a medieval site, a public hall and a popular pub overlooking the river.

Mill Inn, Mungrisdale

Blencathra is the valley's most dominent feature. Beyond Scales there's some awesome close ups from the road of the mountain's soaring ridges.

The village of Threlkeld sits in the shadow of Blencathra and is now bypassed by the A66. You can take the village road at the eastern end and rejoin the main highway at the western.

Keswick is four miles further on, with great views of St John's in the Vale, Blencathra and Skiddaw along the way, making a fitting climax to the tour.

Scales, a scattered collection of roadside dwellings and the White Horse Inn, clings to the lower slopes of Blencathra on the old road from Threlkeld. The road is now part of the Coast to Coast (C2C) cycle route, snaking past the front door of the Inn, a popular pit stop for thirsty cyclists and walkers alike.

There are tremendous views across the valley to Clough Head, St John's in the Vale and the former Threlkeld quarry.

White Horse Inn, Scales

Evening shadows on Blencathra

PIT STOPS

Mill Inn, Mungrisdale
Serves local seasonal produce with fresh fish from the Cumbrian coast. A stone mill-wheel props up the bar and a beer garden overlooks the river. There's a wide range of drinks for thirsty walkers and climbers, including water bowls for dogs. Parking and six cosy rooms to let.
robinsonsbrewery.com

White Horse Inn, Scales
A quintessential country pub boasting flagged floors, open fires, great food, local ales and a warm welcome. Located on the lower slopes of Blencathra and close to Sharp Edge, paths to the mountains start at the pub beer garden.
Two of the old stables have been converted to bunkhouses, which can sleep up to 46 people, with showers, a kitchen and central heating.
thewhitehorse-blencathra.co.uk

6 Threlkeld

In the early 20th century Threlkeld enjoyed a short-lived boom when lead and copper were mined in the valley and granite was quarried from the southern hillsides. Waste from the mines was used to build the characteristic terraced houses in the village.

Since being by-passed by the A66, Threlkeld has become quietly residential and a starting point for many routes up Blencathra, the magnificent mountain on its back doorstep.

Threlkeld Quarry opened on the slopes of Clough Head opposite Blencathra in the 1870s, providing granite for railway ballast, kerb stones and the construction of many local projects, including Thirlmere dam. After closing in 1982 the site was taken over by the Quarry and Mining Museum.

Central Threlkeld & the Public Room

Blencathra dominates the village like a friendly giant. Its glorious trio of spurs, narrow ridges when they leave the shattered scree of the main mountain, spread to substantial buttresses where they become the fields of the village.

Wainwright suggests 12 different routes to the summit, with a constant stream of climbers taking up the challenge. Some even cross Blencathra's scariest ridge, Sharp Edge.

PIT STOPS

Horse & Farrier Inn
Former 17th-century coaching inn with a 1688 datestone above the door. Recently extensively renovated to classy 21st-century standards with en-suite rooms. Slate-flagged floors, beamed ceilings and open fire. Award-winning restaurant serves local and seasonal produce. More gastro-pub than pub-grub.
horseandfarrier.com

The Sally Inn
17th-century sister to the nearby Horse and Farrier. Flag stone floors, oak beams, roaring log fires and en-suite rooms. Dog friendly. *thesalutation.co.uk*

Threlkeld coffee shop
Established in 2014 when the Public Room, built in 1901, was renovated and extended thanks largely to Lottery funding. Light lunches, home baked cakes, sandwiches and soups. Outside area with great views. Run by the villagers.
threlkeldvillagehall.org/coffee-shop

Horse & Farrier Inn

From 1865 to 1972, the Penrith to Cockermouth railway crossed the south side of the valley and continued through the lovely Greta Valley into Keswick. When the line was dismantled the route was turned into a popular footpath.

In 2015, Storm Desmond turned the River Greta into a raging torrent destroying many of the iconic railway bridges. After years of temporary repairs, a £7.9 million renovation reopened the route for cyclists and walkers in 2020.

ATTRACTION

Threlkeld Quarry & Mining Museum
Open-air industrial history museum run by volunteers focusing on the local mining industry. Indoor displays of artefacts and minerals with an impressive outdoor collection of vintage excavators and quarry machinery. Guided tours down a recreated lead and copper mine, plus rides on a narrow-gauge railway into the disused quarry.
threlkeldquarryandminingmuseum.co.uk

The Sally Inn

TOUR 7

Lakeland Drama • 36 miles

Ambleside – Little Langdale – Wrynose Pass – Cockley Beck – Hardknott Pass – Boot – Eskdale Green – Santon Bridge – Wastwater – Wasdale Head – Gosforth

This is a tour of contrasts, up and down, dramatic and tranquil. It's also big on superlatives as we traverse England's steepest road, visit the deepest lake and smallest church, see the highest mountain and have a drink in the bar of the world's greatest liar. In addition, we can imagine life in the remarkably situated Roman fort on Hardknott Pass and reflect on some ancient Viking artifacts at Gosforth. What's more we travel down Eskdale, many people's favourite Lakeland valley, where 'La'arl Ratty', England's oldest and longest narrow gauge railway, transports visitors through the spectacular scenery.

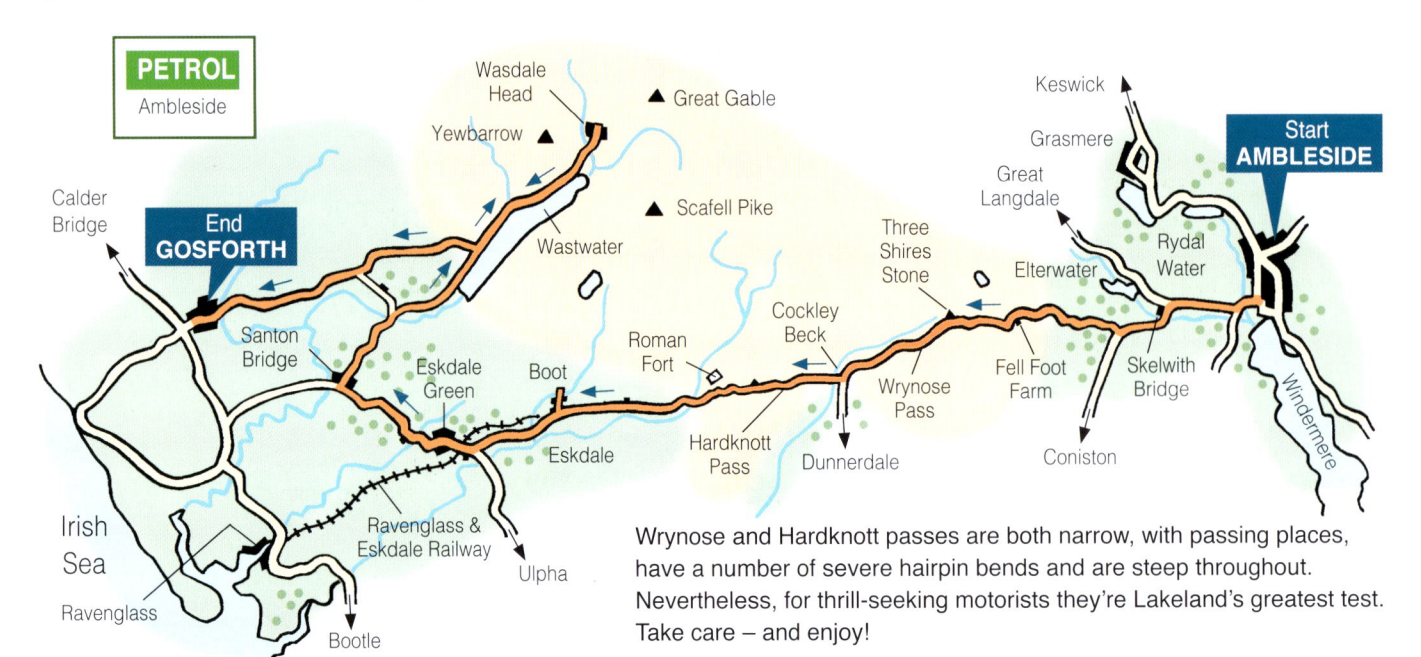

Wrynose and Hardknott passes are both narrow, with passing places, have a number of severe hairpin bends and are steep throughout. Nevertheless, for thrill-seeking motorists they're Lakeland's greatest test. Take care – and enjoy!

The Tour

Begin on the A593 road heading west out of Ambleside, signed Coniston. Keep on this road through Skelwith Bridge (details in Tour 4) and around a mile further on turn right onto an unclassified road signed Wrynose & Elterwater, which twists sharply downhill into light woodland.

Cross the river at the bottom of the hill and take the next turn left, signed Little Langdale and Wrynose. A sign warns 'Extreme Caution' while crossing Wrynose & Hardknott passes ahead. The narrow road passes through a half mile of woodland before the aspect opens and the lovely valley of Little Langdale is spread out to your left. Scattered white houses dot the green rolling fields and a dramatic mountain profile beckons ahead.

Beyond the Three Shires Inn twist around Little Langdale Tarn and soon cross a cattle grid at the junction with the road from Great Langdale. The way ahead is signed Wrynose Pass & Eskdale with a warning sign promising 'Narrow route, severe bends and gradients of up to 30%'.

The next mile or so becomes increasingly wilder with Fell Foot Farm being the last human habitation until Cockley Beck, some three miles distant on the Eskdale side of the pass. Swing sharply left and the route begins to climb steeply beneath Castle Howe (see Tour 4) into the hills.

Cottages in Little Langdale

Fell Foot Farm and the Langdale Pikes

The Passes

Wrynose and Hardknott passes were established in the first century AD by the Romans as part of a supply route between Ambleside and their port at Ravenglass. Whether chariots ever used the route is a matter for conjecture, but the steep, twisting and mainly single lane roads are a considerable challenge for today's visitors.

With 30% gradients in places Hardknott is usually cited as the steepest road in England. Also alarming for modern travellers is when they discover there's no phone signal.

Lakeland Drama — 7

7

Notoriously steep and narrow, Wrynose twists and climbs to a 1281ft-high plateau summit, where there's parking and the Three Shires Stone that used to mark the meeting point of the boundaries of Lancashire, Cumberland.

Note that there are parts of the ascent where it's impossible for two vehicles to pass, though passing places are provided. Rule of the road gives right of way to those ascending, but not everyone agrees! You may have to reverse up or down steep slopes with restricted vision.

The descent to Cockley Beck is more twisty but less steep than the Langdale side. There's also a great view ahead to the head of the Duddon valley and Hardknott Pass – if your nerves will allow a quick glance.

Cross the packhorse bridge over the infant River Duddon and the climb up Hardknott Pass begins.

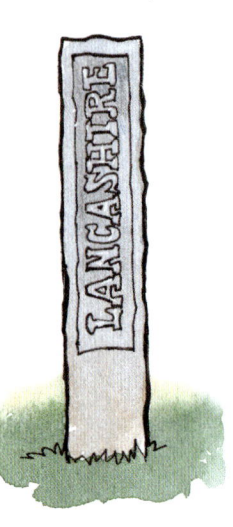

Cockley Beck is a small hamlet historically part of Lancashire. Established in the 16th century, it was closely associated with the mining of copper ore. The farmhouse, built in the 1860s and now a National Trust property, has a self-catering holiday cottage attached for hideaway holidays.

The delightful Duddon Valley spreads south to the Duddon Sands at Foxfield. Without a lake and difficult to access, it's well off the tourist trail but much loved and praised by Lakeland 'purists'. Wordsworth was a fan, writing 34 sonnets about the valley and its river.

The Three Shires Stone

The descent of Wrynose Pass to Cockley Beck

Cockley Beck

Hardknott begins quite sedately but soon steepens, twisting around hairpin bends on exposed sections to quicken the heartbeat. There's a cairn on the 1,291ft summit and parking places on the Eskdale side.

As if the crazy zig zags and other motorists aren't enough, you also have to keep a look out for cyclists, joggers, walkers and stray sheep. The middle part of the descent is fairly level before a steep and twisting plunge into Eskdale.

Things become more relaxed at the small car park near the Roman Fort on the western slopes of Hard Knott fell. The rest is straightforward, with a cattle grid marking the boundary between the mountains and the green fields of upper Eskdale.

Hardknott Roman Fort

With a view down Eskdale to the coast and high crags to the east, Hardknott Fort is superbly positioned to defend the route.

It's worth the short stroll from the car park for a look at the lower walls of the 360 foot square remains. Not all of them are Roman work, some are reconstructions to indicate scale. The views, however, are genuine – and stunning.

The Scafells from the Roman Fort

Hardknott Pass from the Roman Fort

95

7

Lakeland Drama

Another pleasant mile or so brings you to the welcoming Woolpack Inn, where you can relax and boast about your exploits over the passes with other intrepid motorists.

A further mile or so down the road is Brook House Inn, which stands at the junction with the short road to the enchanting hamlet of Boot. Nearby is Dalegarth Station, the terminus of the Ravenglass & Eskdale Railway, more famously known locally as 'La'arl Ratty'.

Eskdale has a subtle charm often missed by the mainstream visitor and daytripper. This is a quiet dale, without showy fells – or a lake – but it does have a beautiful river that twists and winds between woodland, floodplains and miniature gorges. Ancient houses peep from straggly coppices and on each side the fells rise steeply, broken by outcrops of grey rock. Generally, though, they don't dominate the valley.

The exception is Harter Fell in middle Eskdale, an almost perfect cone and a true mountain, rising to 2,143ft high. A series of rocky steps makes it look interesting but don't detract from the overall symmetry. It has often been described as the most beautiful fell in Lakeland, but there is lots of competition.

Brook House Inn

John Ruskin called Eskdale 'The gateway to Paradise', though he was prone to hyperbole. Alfred Wainwright's more measured appraisal was 'A perfect Arcadia in the hills – the finest of all valleys'.

Woolpack Inn & The Hardknott Bar

PIT STOPS

Brook House Inn
Family-run hotel/pub/restaurant. Seven hotel-style bedrooms with en suite. Friendly local staff. Menu a step up from usual pub meals. Big on drinks – local real ales, a shed load of gins and 180 different whiskies. Co hosts of the annual Boot Beer Festival. Terrific rural views.
brookhouseinn.co.uk

Woolpack Inn
Historic hostelry with seven en-suite and comfy rooms. Huge range of food from bar meals in the Woolpack Café to gourmet choices in the restaurant. Cool public bar with wooden floors and woodburner. Local real ales and a large beer garden. Co-hosts of the annual Boot Beer Festival. Dog friendly
woolpack.co.uk

Boot

Spread along a *cul de sac* off the main road and with a name who's derivation appears to have defeated numerous experts, the oddly-titled hamlet of Boot cries out for exploration.

Beginning in 1870 and for around 40 years this was a mining village. Iron ore was mined from both north and south of the river but by 1912 both mines had been abandoned.

A terrace of white-painted former miners cottages leads to a collection of 500 year-old cottages, converted to desirable twenty-first century holiday lets. A nearby packhorse bridge crosses Whillan Beck to the watermill and a bridleway heads up the fellside.

Here packhorse trails once crossed, the corpse road to Wasdale began and the railway from the coast ended at the mine workings on Boot Bank.

The packhorse bridge, watermill and slopes of Boot Bank

ATTRACTION
Eskdale Mill

Dating from 1578, the mill is a rare survivor of a traditional watermill and drying kiln. It's the last remaining working water-powered corn mill in the Lake District National Park. Cumbria County Council restored the mill in the 1970s and in 2006 a group of local people took it over to preserve its historical fabric and run it as a visitor attraction.
eskdalemill.co.uk

Boot Inn

PIT STOP
Boot Inn

Family-run hotel and restaurant in the village. Seven bedrooms, most en suite. Quality, award-winning pub meals. Dog friendly.
thebooteskdale.co.uk

7

Lakeland Drama

The road continues west between the railway and the River Esk to a junction at the King George IV Inn. Turn right, signed Ravenglass 7. Cross the railway bridge at The Green railway station and enter sleepy Eskdale Green.

Just beyond the village cross the River Mite to the Bowerhouse Inn. A further couple of miles through peaceful meadows and woodland brings you to a T-junction at Santon Bridge. The inn stands by the river and there's a large campsite nearby. Our route turns right here onto a minor road, signed Wasdale 2¼ miles.

King George IV Inn

La'arl Ratty at Muncaster Mill station

La'arl Ratty

First opened as a three-foot gauge in 1875, the railway carried iron ore from the mines in Eskdale to Ravenglass, seven miles away.
The mines and the railway both went bust but the line struggled on until 1913, when it was dismantled.

Two years later it was relaid to a tiny 15-inch gauge with steam trains carrying goods, passengers and mail. After the First World War, granite quarries reopened in the valley and for a while the line became industrial again. But with the closure of the quarries in 1953 a decline set in.

In 1960 the railway was bought at auction by a preservation society and turned into a popular visitor attraction with five working steam locomotives and seven request stops along the valley.

The Ravenglass & Eskdale Railway is one of the oldest and longest narrow gauge railways in England, known affectionately as La'al Ratty.

PIT STOP

King George IV Inn
A traditional inn near The Green railway station. It's a welcoming pub with open fire, oak ceilings and slate floors. Sunny patio outside. Dog friendly.
kinggeorge-eskdale.co.uk

Eskdale Green

This small and peaceful settlement, with a village shop, is attractively set on the lower slopes of Muncaster Fell. Many of the houses are built of Eskdale granite, the most handsome of Lakeland rock with a fabulous sparkle in shades of pink and blue.

Bower House Inn

Village shop

Part of the Outward Bound Gate House estate

Santon Bridge Inn

In 1896, two large country houses with extensive grounds, woods and a private lake were built in the village for the Rea family. They were sold In 1949 to the Outward Bound Trust, an educational charity developing young peoples attitudes and behaviour through adventures in the wild, which converted the estate to their Eskdale Centre.

PIT STOPS

Bower House Inn
A former 17th-century coaching inn, the Bower House combines traditional Lake District hospitality with modern comforts such as wifi and regular events. Food and ales are locally sourced. 20 bedrooms. Dog friendly with a large beer garden bowerhouseinn.com

Santon Bridge Inn
Famous for its Sunday lunches, good food and hospitality, the inn also boasts open fires, real ale and 16 individual ensuite rooms. In November it hosts the renowned World's Biggest Liar Competition. Licensed for civil marriage ceremonies.
santonbridgeinn.com

Oddly the road swings right here out of Eskdale into the broad vale of the river Mite, Miterdale. The railway also follows this route, so the Eskdale Railway line actually spends more time in Miterdale than it does in Eskdale!

7

Continue for a couple of miles to Cinderdale Bridge, which crosses the River Irt. The hamlet of Nether Wasdale is close by but our route turns right here, signed Wasdale Head & The Lake. Wastwater is only a mile away but hidden from view by a thick patch of woodland. As you emerge from the trees, the sudden first sight of the wonderful mountain desolation around the lake can be overwhelming. There are places to park to fully appreciate the dramatic scenery.

The road from Santon Bridge climbs to a fabulous panoramic view of the Wasdale mountains ahead. From Cinderdale Bridge there's a string of classic Lakeland landscapes: woodland, open fields, sheep, bracken and stone walls. Half-timbered Wasdale Hall, a youth centre, is hidden in the trees at the lake foot.

The Cinderdale Bridge turn

Wastwater

The deepest, most dramatic and most haunting of all the lakes, Wastwater has an almost total absence of trees to break up its stark outline, stripping the dark waters of all trace of prettiness. It's around three miles long and a half mile wide. And it's deep. Very deep.

Overshadowing the lake, in every sense, are the awesome Wastwater Screes, an almost 2,000ft high wall of sharp and shattered rock, tumbling in a series of fan-shaped downslopes to the lake bed 259ft below the surface.

Slopes of Middle Fell

Bowderdale

Yewbarrow 2,060ft (628m)

Mosedale

Great Gable 2,949ft (899m)

Wasdale Head

The classic mountain composition at the head of the valley – Yewbarrow, Great Gable and Lingmell – was for a while adopted as the emblem of the National Park. Scafell Pike, England's highest mountain, is rightly dominent with Scafell providing a knobbly counterpoint.

Up to 4,000,000 gallons of water a day are piped from the lake to the Sellafield nuclear facility as an 'industrial water supply'.

7

Lakeland Drama

Illgill Head
1,998ft (609m)

Lingmell
2,649ft (807m)

Lingmell Gill

Scafell Pike
3,209ft (978m)

Scafell Crag

Scafell
3,163ft (964m)

The Screes

sty Head

Wastwater

The narrow road, unfenced for much of the way, follows the shore for around two and a half miles to the head of the lake. Another mile of so brings you to the road's end at Wasdale Head, where there's parking.

Return along the lakeside and turn right at the junction, signed Gosforth. Pass through Greendale, a huddle of dwellings gathered beneath mighty Bull Crag, before enjoying a peaceful and picturesque four miles or so to end this tour in the hospitable village of Gosforth.

Wasdale Head

The handful of permanent buildings is hardly a village but at the height of summer the population of Wasdale Head balloons to more than that of some small towns. British rock climbing began on the surrounding high crags and with England's highest mountain, deepest lake, smallest church and the original world's biggest liar to be found in this tranquil corner of the Lake District, it's also the home of superlatives.

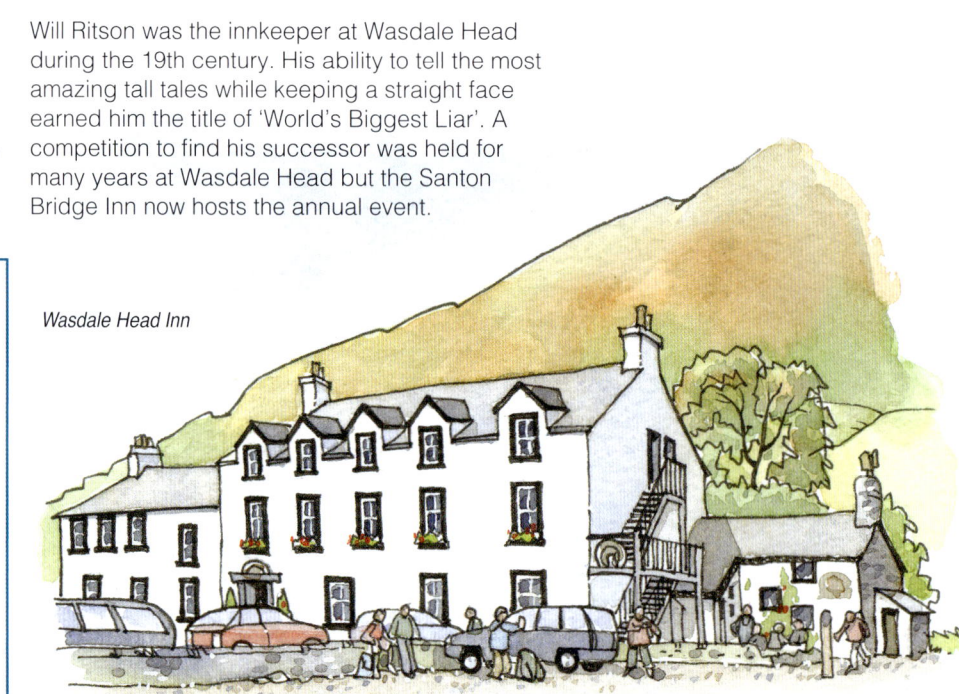

Will Ritson was the innkeeper at Wasdale Head during the 19th century. His ability to tell the most amazing tall tales while keeping a straight face earned him the title of 'World's Biggest Liar'. A competition to find his successor was held for many years at Wasdale Head but the Santon Bridge Inn now hosts the annual event.

Wasdale Head Inn

Wasdale Head Inn

Still the Lakeland climber's unofficial HQ. The famous Ritson's Bar has wooden booths and benches, and serves wholesome food and real ale. The main building offers nine compact guest rooms, plus three 'superior' rooms in the adjacent cottage. There's also six self-catering apartments in a converted barn. Upmarket meals are served in the restaurant.
Outdoor seating areas. A small shop nearby sells 'all you need to go out on the fells', plus advice on routes etc.
wasdale.com

St Olaf's church is indeed small but it's tag of 'smallest' is an ongoing controversy. The building is over 400 year old, built of rendered Wasdale stones and protected from the weather by 32 yew trees. It's wooden roof beams are said to have come from wrecked Viking ships. It's a delightful place, though with all the unpolished woodwork it has been unkindly likened to a cowshed.

In the little churchyard there are memorials to climbers, killed on Scafell, Gable and the Himalayas.

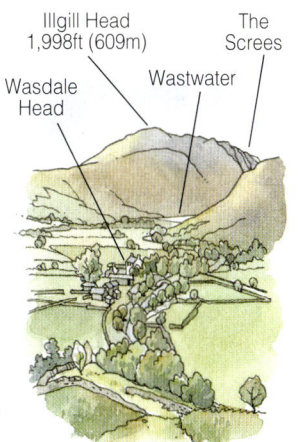

Wasdale from Kirk Fell

Stones, washed down from the fellsides, are are all over Upper Wasdale. Farmers have collected some into great heaps in the fields. Those that haven't been worn smooth have been built into high, substantial walls. The valley's remarkable pattern of walled fields is most impressive when seen from the fellsides above.

7

Lakeland Drama

St Olaf's Church

Apart from all its other claims to fame, Wasdale is also home to the World's greatest fell runner, Joss Naylor. His speciality is running up and down as many fells as he can in a given time. Such as an astonishing 72 summits in less than 24 hours. You only have to look around to see how difficult that is.

Greendale & Bull Crag

103

7 Gosforth

After the drama earlier in the tour, peaceful Gosforth is quite a contrast. Though often dismissed as only a commuter village for the Sellafied nuclear plant a couple of miles away, the village is surprisingly large and hospitable with an interesting Viking heritage. Houses in the main street are typically West Cumbrian, plain, unfussy and straightforward. Set in open countryside and close to the coast, it has a reputation for fresh breezes.

There's an excellent village store with a café, one or two gift shops and a number of pubs, three of them facing one another across the village centre. Various local hotels also boast bars, beer gardens and restaurants.

The Globe, one of the village centre inns

The village centre with the Globe, Lion & Lamb and Wheatsheaf inns.

Town Hall & library

Gosforth's greatest treasure is the 11th-century cross in St Mary's churchyard. The slender, 14ft-high sandstone cross is carved with a mixture of Viking and Christian symbols. It's the tallest ancient cross in England and considered to be of great importance as it displays the transition from pagen to Christian beliefs.

The Gosforth Cross

St Mary's Church dates from 1789, built on the foundations of a 12th-century building. Two 10th-century Norse hogback tombstones in the knave were uncovered in a Victorian 'improvement' in 1896.

A cork tree in the churchyard, planted in 1833, is claimed to be the most northerly surviving one in Europe. The tool-shed is built of stones from the original church, and is now a listed building.

The quirky town hall and library dates back to 1628, the oldest building in the village.

More recent is the 19th-century Steelfield Hall on the village outskirts, built in 1840 for Humphrey Senhouse. A landowner and High Sheriff, he founded the port of Maryport and was married to Mary, an heiress and the daughter of the Bishop of Carlisle.

St Mary's Church

PIT STOPS

Gosforth Bakery
Hugely popular takeaway on the main street, Whiteway. Pies, bread, cakes, quiche, sausage rolls etc, all home-baked daily. Also pie and peas, breakfast boxes, salad boxes, etc; to order.
Phone 019467 25525

The Lion & Lamb
A recently upgraded traditional village inn with darts, dominoes and pool. Plus outside seating, live music, pub grub, Sky/BT Sports, local real ales and 13 rooms to let.
thelionthelamb.co.uk.

Gosforth Hall
Dating back to 1658, Gosforth Hall is now an upmarket hotel and restaurant with 17 ensuite rooms and a reputation for cooking perfect pub classics in its lounge, bar and restaurant. Al fresco dining in the beer garden, one of best in the area, providing a Mediterranean feel to the Lake District.
gosforthhall.co.uk

7

Lakeland Drama

105

TOUR 8 — Lakeland Icons • 30 miles

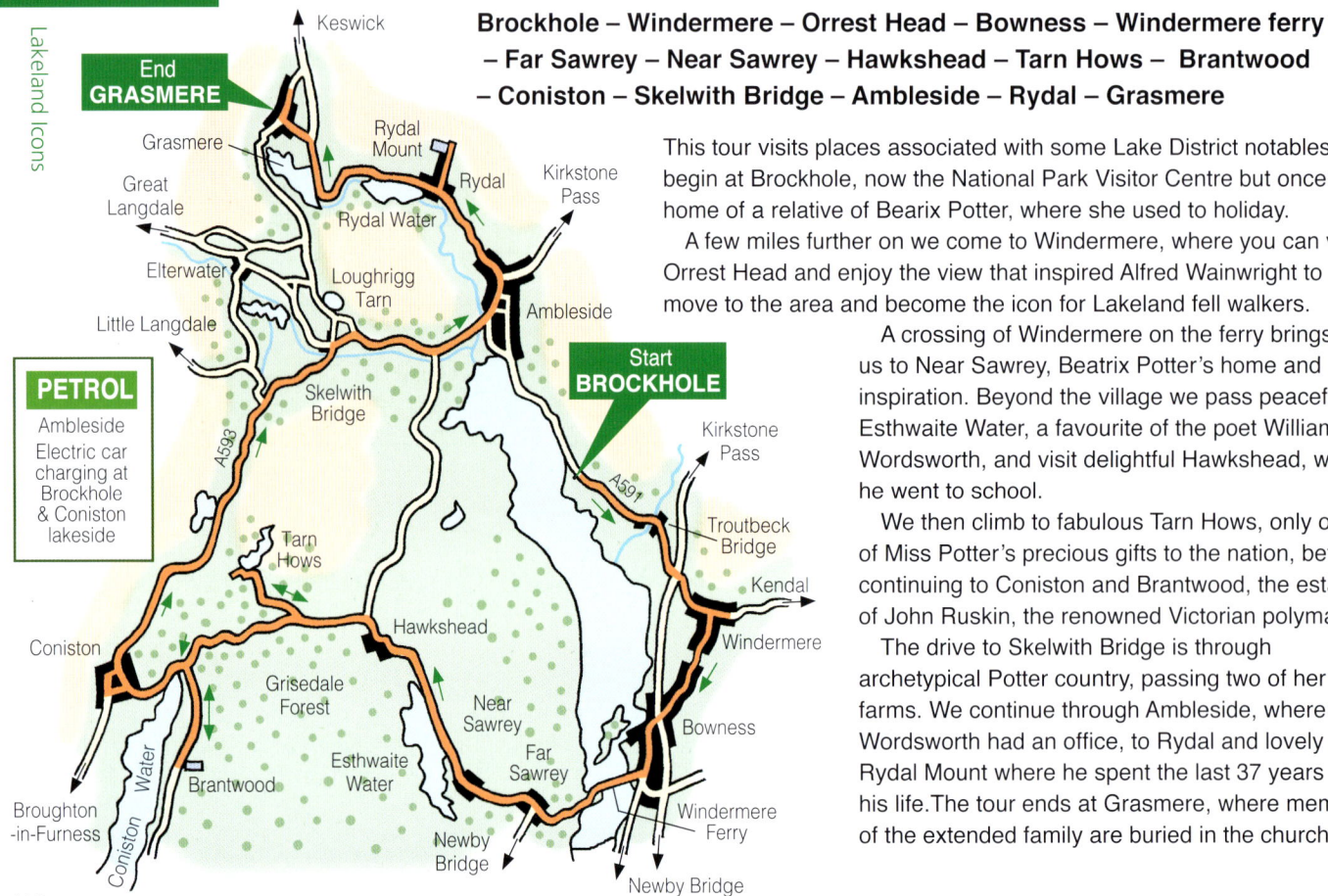

Brockhole – Windermere – Orrest Head – Bowness – Windermere ferry – Far Sawrey – Near Sawrey – Hawkshead – Tarn Hows – Brantwood – Coniston – Skelwith Bridge – Ambleside – Rydal – Grasmere

Start: BROCKHOLE
End: GRASMERE

PETROL
Ambleside
Electric car charging at Brockhole & Coniston lakeside

This tour visits places associated with some Lake District notables. We begin at Brockhole, now the National Park Visitor Centre but once the home of a relative of Bearix Potter, where she used to holiday.

A few miles further on we come to Windermere, where you can visit Orrest Head and enjoy the view that inspired Alfred Wainwright to move to the area and become the icon for Lakeland fell walkers.

A crossing of Windermere on the ferry brings us to Near Sawrey, Beatrix Potter's home and inspiration. Beyond the village we pass peaceful Esthwaite Water, a favourite of the poet William Wordsworth, and visit delightful Hawkshead, where he went to school.

We then climb to fabulous Tarn Hows, only one of Miss Potter's precious gifts to the nation, before continuing to Coniston and Brantwood, the estate of John Ruskin, the renowned Victorian polymath.

The drive to Skelwith Bridge is through archetypical Potter country, passing two of her farms. We continue through Ambleside, where Wordsworth had an office, to Rydal and lovely Rydal Mount where he spent the last 37 years of his life. The tour ends at Grasmere, where members of the extended family are buried in the churchyard.

🚗 The Tour

Start at the National Park Visitor Centre, Brockhole. Entrance to the centre is free, though there is a charge for parking.

Continue along the A591 to Windermere where you can park and maybe take a stroll up to Orrest Head where the young Alfred Wainwright first saw the view that changed his life.

Brockhole

Built at the end of the 19th century, Brockhole House was a holiday home for a wealthy silk merchant William Gaddum and his wife Edith (née) Potter, cousin to Beatrix Potter. It was designed by architect Dan Gibson with gardens created by renowned landscape designer Thomas Mawson. Brockhole is acclaimed as one of the lesser known Arts & Crafts treasures of Cumbria. Gaddum selected a superb plot of land for his 'summer house'. Set high on the terraced gardens, the house offers spectacular views across Windermere to the Langdale Pikes, Pike of Stickle and Harrison Stickle.

After Gaddum died in 1966 Brockhole was sold and has undergone many changes since. For a time it was a rural convalescent home for Merseyside Hospital Board. The Lake District National Park Authority purchased the house and grounds in 1966, opening it in 1969 as the UK's first National Park Visitor Centre. Some of the most significant development and restoration at Brockhole has taken place in recent years with a Lottery funded major refurbishment in 1998. The Gaddum Gallery was opened in 2016, and the Kitchen Garden Project completed in 2019.

Apart from providing information on the Lake District generally, there's always something going on here. Take your pick from boat hire, kayak tours, krazi carts, laser clay shooting, archery, bike hire, mini golf, adventure playground, treetop nets and treks, trails and orienteering, etc, etc.

You can also charge your electric car.

Brockhole

Windermere town

Most English towns began with a market charter. Windermere began with a railway station. It opened in 1848 when the line arrived at the hamlet of Birthwaite, which rapidly developed into a holiday town and eventually adopted the the station name of Windermere. The local company of Pattinsons built the station and at the same time constructed the splendid Windermere Hotel that overlooks the station and the town.

By the 1960s few visitors arrived by train and in 1976 one line was taken up leaving only a single track to Oxenholme. The large station was abandoned in 1983.

A year later it re-opened as Booth's supermarket with some of the station features incorporated. A new £90,000 station, built of wood in the Furness Railway fashion, was opened in 1985 paid for by a joint BR and local action group effort.

Windermere suffers from a surfeit of traffic, all seemingly going somewhere else. Indeed the town appears to discourage motorists stopping, with its only public car park a bewildering maze of tight corners in the local library garden. A pity really as the town's central area is worth exploring as its Victorian architecture and traditional shops lend it an agreeable old-fashioned appeal.

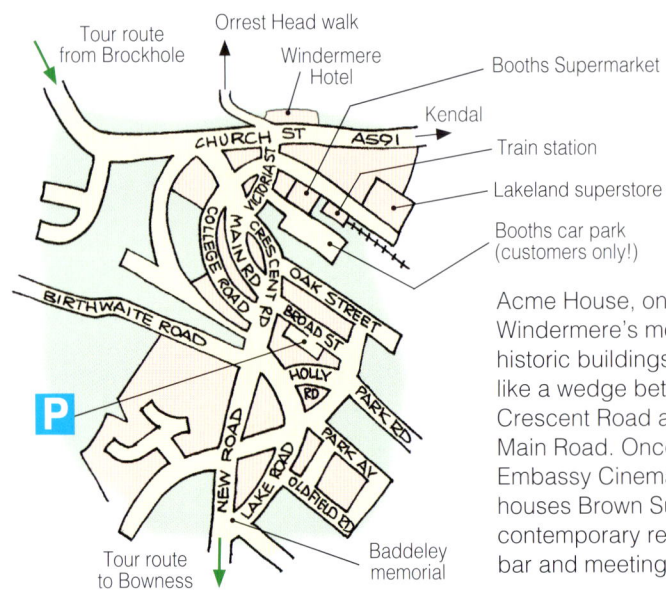

Acme House, one of Windermere's most historic buildings thrusts like a wedge between Crescent Road and Main Road. Once the Embassy Cinema it now houses Brown Sugar, a contemporary restaurant, bar and meeting place.

Brown Sugar

Victorian buildings and modern shopfronts

Lakeland is a truly lakeland success story, starting in the 1960s with the three Raynor brothers helping their dad count packs of plastic bags. Decades of development led to today's company, still with the same three brothers at the helm and with 70 stores throughout the country employing some 1,500 people. Fitting then that their flagship store is in Windermere, where it all began.

Lakeland

Baddeley Clock

The Baddeley Clock marks the official division between Windermere and Bowness. It was built as a memorial to Mountford John Byrde Baddeley (1843 - 1906) who wrote a series of well-regarded walker's routes starting from the then new town of Windermere.

PIT STOPS

Windermere has a huge range of eateries. Here are a few suggestions:.

First Floor Cafe
Situated in Lakeland's flagship store. Serves breakfast and brunch. Wide range of coffees, teas and freshly baked cakes. Also full meals with a drink.
firstfloorcafe.co.uk

Brown Sugar
A Dutton Cuisine restaurant and bar with a huge range of drinks and food available. Three floors of contempory design and quirky features. Heated outside terrace. Watch the traffic crawl by from the first floor balcony.
dutton-cuisine.co.uk/brownsugar

Sugar & Spice Café & Bistro
Family-run and friendly, serving traditional afternoon tea, freshly ground coffee, loose leaf tea, homemade cakes & scones, fresh sandwiches and main meals. Licensed.
Phone 015394 22979

8 Lakeland Icons

Lakeland Icons

Orrest Head

'Here the promised land is seen in all its glory' thought the young (aged 23) Alfred Wainwright, and many more inspired by his example have stood here and vowed to climb them all. There are 214 Wainwright summits and the fastest they have all been climbed one after another is in a remarkable six days, 13 hours and one minute.

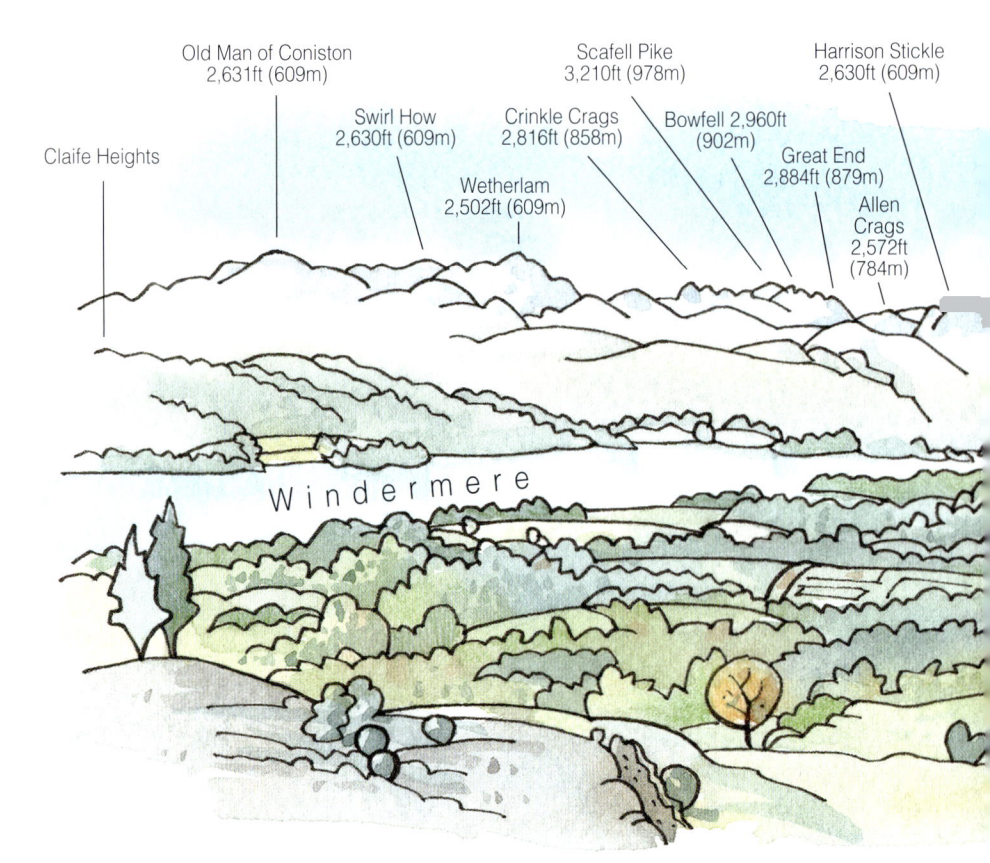

A.W. Wainwright (1907-91)

Blackburn-born Alfred Wainwright left school at thirteen, but after years of study qualified as a municipal accountant. Inspired by the view from Orrest Head when he first saw it in 1930, he yearned to live near the fells. The move to Kendal came in 1941, where he eventually became Borough Treasurer.

His accounts of walks up the fells were initially just for his own amusement but in 1955 he decided to self-publish them. His classic seven Pictorial Guides were completed between 1955 and 1966, all written and drawn in his own hand, He went on to write and illustrate over 40 books, about Lakeland, Scotland and Wales.

Despite a dislike of publicity, in later life he began to appear on television and even Desert Island Discs on radio. He also wrote coffee-table books to support animal charities. The sales from all his books have been estimated to exceed £4 million.

Claife Heights

Old Man of Coniston 2,631ft (609m)
Swirl How 2,630ft (609m)
Wetherlam 2,502ft (609m)
Crinkle Crags 2,816ft (858m)
Scafell Pike 3,210ft (978m)
Bowfell 2,960ft (902m)
Great End 2,884ft (879m)
Harrison Stickle 2,630ft (609m)
Allen Crags 2,572ft (784m)

Windermere

The record was achieved by Steve Birkinshaw in June 2014. Wainwright himself took a more leisurely pace. Sadly, considering its importance in triggering the great Wainwright walk to iconic status, Orrest Head, with a summit rising only to around 783ft, is not listed amongst the blessed 214.

However, the inoffensive nobble of rock is pleasant enough and does appear in AW's *Outlying Fells of Lakeland* where he suggests a round trip, up and down from Windermere train station of about one hour. The view is worth spending some more time with, and remarkable not only for its picturesque distinction but also how little it has changed since Wainwright first came here in 1930.

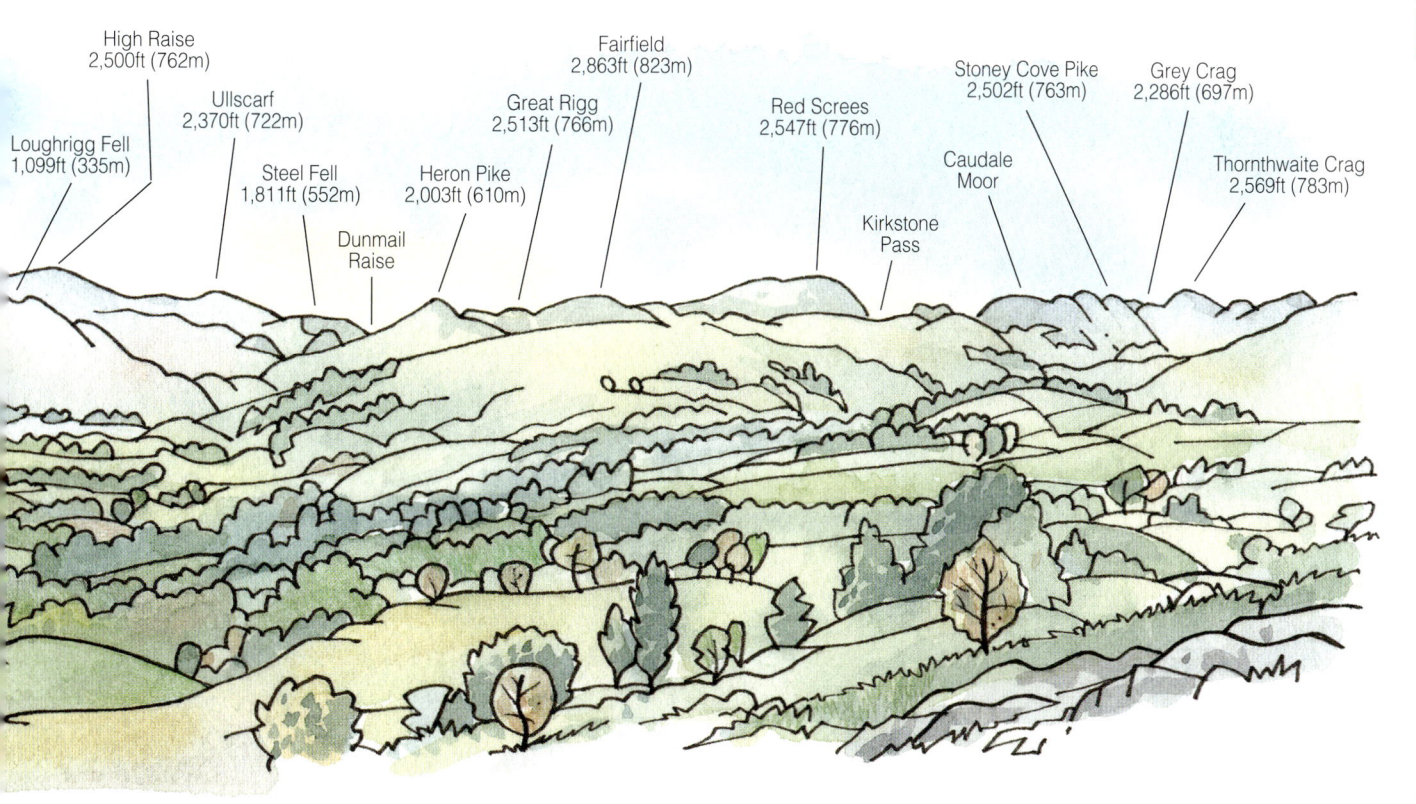

8 Lakeland Icons

High Raise 2,500ft (762m)
Ullscarf 2,370ft (722m)
Loughrigg Fell 1,099ft (335m)
Steel Fell 1,811ft (552m)
Dunmail Raise
Heron Pike 2,003ft (610m)
Fairfield 2,863ft (823m)
Great Rigg 2,513ft (766m)
Red Screes 2,547ft (776m)
Kirkstone Pass
Stoney Cove Pike 2,502ft (763m)
Caudale Moor
Grey Crag 2,286ft (697m)
Thornthwaite Crag 2,569ft (783m)

8 Lakeland Icons

Carry on down Lake Road to Bowness, where there's a number of car parks, often quickly filled in summer.

After sampling the delights of the vibrant lakeside town take the ferry across Windermere to Sawrey. You may have to queue at holiday times. An alternative is to drive on to Newby Bridge at the foot of the lake, then take the narrow road along the west side of the lake to Far Sawrey. Near Sawrey is famous as the home of Beatrix Potter.

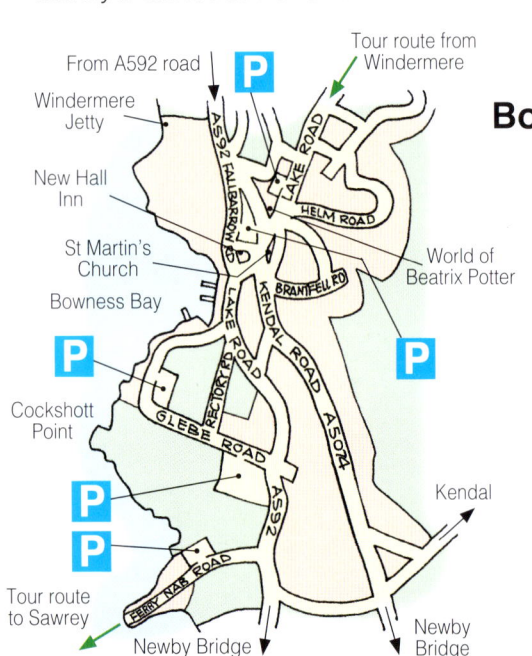

Bowness Bay lake cruise piers

Bowness

Bowness is often unkindly called the 'Blackpool of the Lakes'. On a sunny bank holiday there may be some truth in that as hoards of visitors eager 'for a day in the Lakes' flood into the vibrant lakeside town.

The Vikings originally settled here in the 11th century and until the railway arrived Bowness consisted of little more than a few fisherman's cottages. Easier and quicker access brought tourists and they have never stopped coming since. From lake cruises to gift shops, pubs and fish and chips, there's plenty to amuse them these days but, as cynics often point out, Bowness is hardly representative of the Lake District as a whole.

There's been a ferry across Windermere for at least 500 years, originally large rowing boats. The present ferry, built in 1990 on the Welsh coast, carries 15 vehicles and as the only static ferry across any of the lakes, has become a tourist attraction itself.

Windermere ferry

New Hall Inn

New Hall Inn is locally know as 'Hole int' Wall' from the time when there was a smithy next door and ale was served to the smiths through a hole in the wall. The 17th century inn is one of the original three which stood on the old road through the town.

A church has stood on the site of St Martin's since 1203, although the present building dates from 1436. Medieval glass from Cartmel Priory was brought here for safety during the Dissolution and incorporated into the east window, St Martin's greatest treasure. The churchyard was consecrated during the Great Plague of 1348 and some of the yew trees are over 600 years old. Burials ceased here in 1856.

The World of Beatrix Potter

St Martin's Church

Crag Brow (before the magnificent Chestnut tree in Queen Square was chopped down)

ATTRACTIONS

The World of Beatrix Potter
Devoted to the iconic children's author and illustrator. All her 23 tales are featured in 3D form, complete with sounds and smells. There's virtual walks to the places that inspired her, plus interactive children's attractions, a gift shop, a garden and a themed café.
hop-skip-jump.com

Windermere Jetty: Museum of Boats, Steam and Stories
A collection of 40 beautiful boats covering the history of sailing on Windermere.
windermerejetty.org

PITSTOPS

Bowness is packed with places to eat and drink, from fish & chips at Vinegar Jones to gourmet dinners at Miller Howe. You only need to stroll around to find somewhere to suit your taste and pocket.

Eateries line Ash Street and Church Street and the old area of Lowside is also worth exploring.

113

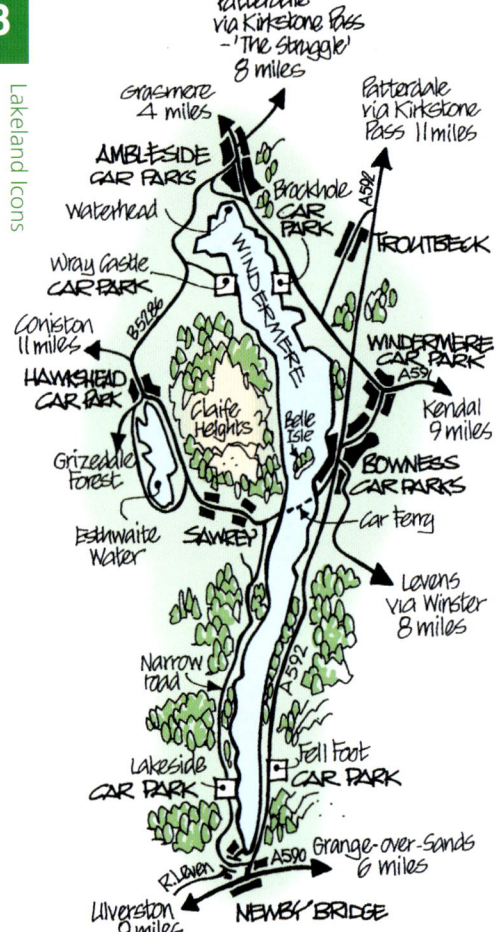

Windermere

As befits England's largest lake, Windermere has a stately air and is named after a Norse hero, Vinandr. The lake is ten and a half miles long and one mile wide, with a maximum depth of 219ft. Belle Isle, the largest of Windermere's 18 islands almost cuts the lake in two at Bowness. In ancient times it was a busy Roman highway and later used to transport Iron ore and charcoal. These days all manner of boats scrummage for a stretch of clear water. Large power boats were effectively banned from the lake when a 10mph speed limit became effective in 2005, which also prohibited water-skiing.

The shoreline is thickly wooded and the eastern side dotted by large mansions, now mostly hotels, built by wealthy Lancashire industrialists. The quieter western side has a narrow road only as far as Sawrey but a lakeside path runs along most of the lakeside.

The Ferry House from Cockshott Point

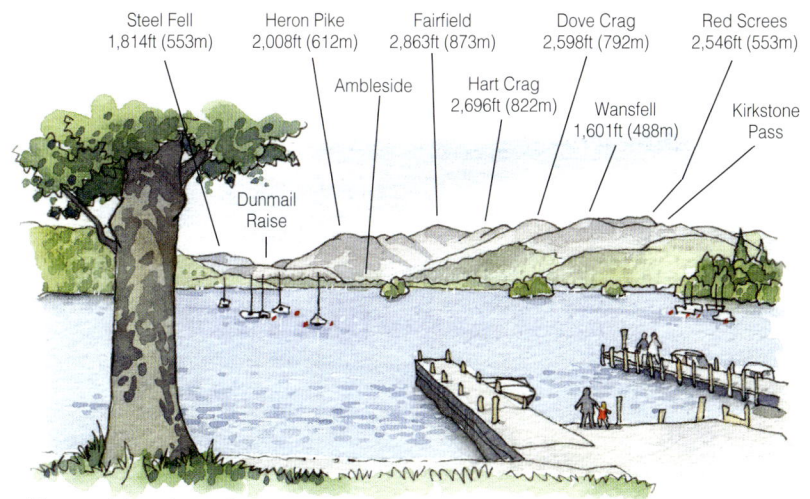

8 Lakeland Icons

View north from the marina

Labels: Steel Fell 1,814ft (553m); Heron Pike 2,008ft (612m); Fairfield 2,863ft (873m); Dove Crag 2,598ft (792m); Red Screes 2,546ft (553m); Dunmail Raise; Ambleside; Hart Crag 2,696ft (822m); Wansfell 1,601ft (488m); Kirkstone Pass

Belsfield Hotel

The Bowness promenade is overlooked by the Belsfield Hotel, the home of HW Schneider in the late 19th century. He used to commute each day to his industrial empire in Barrow, eating breakfast while travelling on his private launch down the lake to Lakeside, then by a special carriage on the Furness Railway to Barrow.

His schedule was reversed in the evening, getting him home in time for dinner at Bowness.

The beautiful house on Belle Isle is said to be the only truly round house in England. The present building dates from 1774 but was ravaged by fire in 1996. It's now restored and inhabited but strictly private. You can, however, catch a glimpse of the house through the trees from Cockshot Point.

Belle Isle House

Windermere lake Cruises operate 17 vessels that sail every day throughout the year. Two of the four largest 'steamers' can carry over 500 passengers and the oldest, *Swan*, dates to 1938.

The latest, *Swift,* was launched in 2020. It was built in the Netherlands, shipped in sections and assembled at the Windermere lakeside.

The Swan *at Bowness*

115

Beatrix Potter (1866-1943)

Born in London to genteel, upper-middle-class Victorians, Beatrix Potter was educated at home, but found an artistic outlet in 'drawing and painting little books for children'.

Family holidays were spent in rented but grand houses in the Lake District, where a family friend, Canon Rawnsley, encouraged her to self-publish using her own money. Her first book, *The Tale of Peter Rabbit*, was published in 1901 with a limited print run. A year later it was republished by Messrs Warne, who went on to handle all her later books. With the money she made from her 'little' books, she bought Hill Top Farm at Near Sawrey in 1905.

At the age of 47, she married William Heelis, a local solicitor, and devoted her life to the preservation of farms and the countryside, becoming a respected expert on Herdwick sheep, the local breed.

When she died in 1943 all her property – fifteen farms with their flocks, many cottages and 4,000 acres of land – was left to the National Trust.

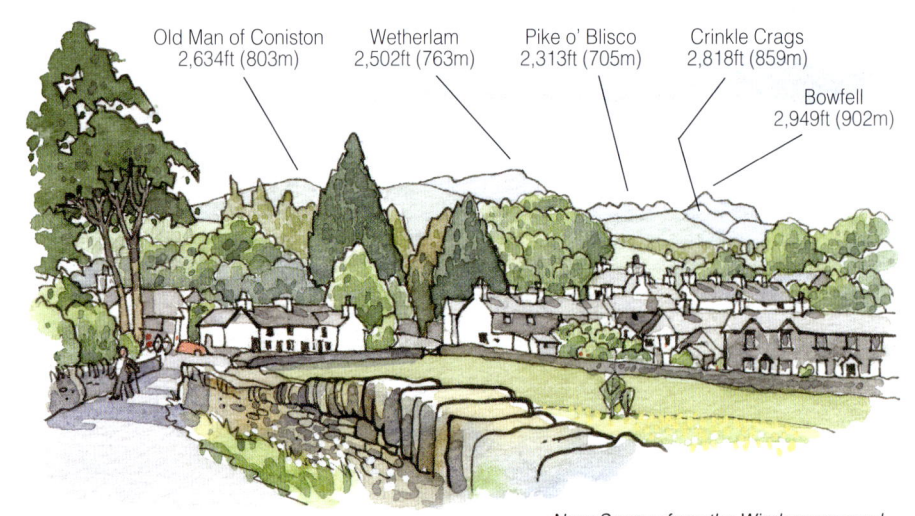

Near Sawrey from the Windermere road

Near Sawrey

Despite the worldwide fame of Beatrix Potter, its most celebrated resident, and the flood of thousands of devotees visiting her house, Hill Top, the hamlet of Near Sawrey hangs on to its dignity and remains the most decorous and unflashy of all the Lakeland honeypots.

The cluster of white-painted traditional cottages nestle in a shallow vale with meadows spreading down the hillside to the quiet lake of Esthwaite Water. Low hills are dotted with woodland, stone walls line the meadows where rabbits hop. It all seems so familiar, so perfect, just as it is in the Potter books. You half expect to meet a duck wearing a mop cap.

Claife Heights, the wooded upland that rises from Sawrey and separates Esthwaite Water from Windermere, has, despite its name, a summit at only around 900ft. Its best feature is a number of attractive tarns, where Beatrix Potter liked to wander. She even kept a boat on one and did some fishing.

Following her purchase of Hill Top Beatrix Potter had an extension built on for her farm manager, while she remained in London caring for her parents. She visited when she could and did some of her best work there.

After marriage she and her husband lived in nearby Castle Farm Cottage, but kept ownership of Hill Top. Country life developed in her a strong belief in the preservation of rural Lakeland, a conviction she shared with Canon Rawnsley, a co-founder of the National Trust.

Motivated by developers buying run-down farms for housing development, she bought several estates over the years believing that they should be kept together as working farm units. They were all left to the Trust in her will, along with Hill Top, with the provision that the house be kept as she had known it and opened to visitors.

Beatrix Potter's greatness is that not only have her books given pleasure to generations of children, she also used the money from those books for the benefit of the country as a whole. It's been said that Peter Rabbit and his friends saved 4,000 acres of southern Lakeland.

Hill Top

Tower Bank Arms (Illustrated in The Tale of Jemima Puddle-Duck*)*

ATTRACTION

Hill Top

Hugely popular. Beatrix Potter's workplace and occasional sleep-over house. Owned and managed by the National Trust, which is very strict on protecting their priceless property. Expect to queue for entry. Limited numbers in the house at one time. Closed on Fridays. No price reductions for parties and coaches not permitted. Limited parking. Still well worth visiting though! *nationaltrust.org.uk/hill-top*

PITSTOP

Tower Bank Arms

Hill Top's adjacent pub, owned by the National Trust. It lives up to the Potter image of oakbeams, slate floors and a cast iron range. Four simple but smart rooms to let. Acclaimed for its wide range of beers and good food, from local lamb to Esthwaite trout. *towerbankarms.co.uk*

Lakeland Icons

8 Lakeland Icons

From Near Sawrey the road continues along the eastern side of Esthwaite Water to Hawkshead, one of the Lakeland's honeypot tourist villages with a huge car park.

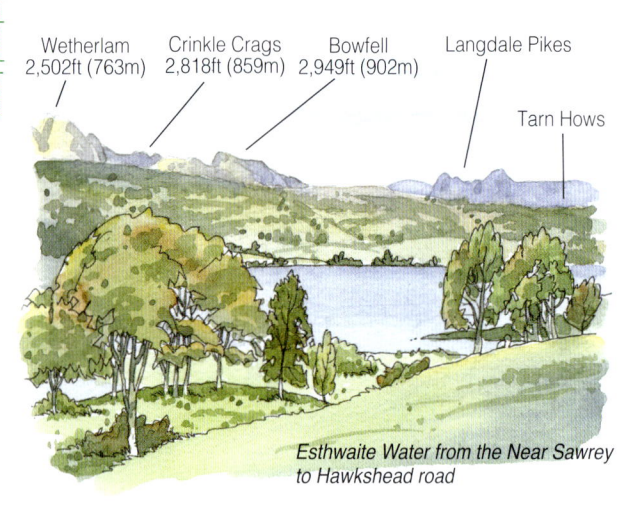

Wetherlam 2,502ft (763m)
Crinkle Crags 2,818ft (859m)
Bowfell 2,949ft (902m)
Langdale Pikes
Tarn Hows

Esthwaite Water from the Near Sawrey to Hawkshead road

Esthwaite Water

Only a modest one and a half miles long, around 700 yards wide and barely 80ft deep, Esthwaite Water is one of smallest and least visited of the region's lakes. The only lakeside access is via a small car park at the southern end.

However, surrounded by low fells, woodland and minor roads, Esthwaite Water is appealingly pretty, with a great view of the Langdale Pikes from the Hawkshead road.

As a schoolboy William Wordsworth knew the lake well, mentioning it three times in his magnum opus, *The Prelude*.

Hawkshead

With the character of a small market town rather than a village, Hawkshead's compact, uncoordinated arrangement of ancient whitewashed buildings, cobbled pavements and squares, and narrow streets with low archways leading to secluded courtyards, is a joy to explore. Hawkshead is unlike any other village (or town) in the Lake District. Also uniquely, it has connections with both William Wordsworth and Beatrix Potter.

The Town Hall

During the 18th and 19th centuries Hawkshead was the administration centre for the area. The Town Hall was built in 1790 and the five open-arched shops at square level were occupied on market days by butchers.

The Beatrix Potter Gallery occupies rooms once used as an office by Potter's solicitor husband, William Heelis. The Heelis law firm had been in the village since 1861 and William became a partner from 1900 until his death in 1945, when the building passed to the National Trust. His office is preserved and the remainder of the gallery is devoted to his wife.

The Beatrix Potter Gallery and Main Street

118

The Grammar School was founded in 1585 by Edward Sandys, a locally-born cleric who Queen Elizabeth made Archbishop of York. William Wordsworth attended the school from 1779-87.

Although Cockermouth born, the boy William, then aged eight, was sent to school at Hawkshead following his mother's death. He lodged in the care of Ann Tyson, first in the village 1779-84, then at Colthouse after the death of Mrs Tyson's husband.

The school is now a museum and library. Star attraction is Wordsworth's school desk – complete with his carved initials – encased in glass.

Ann Tyson's Cottage

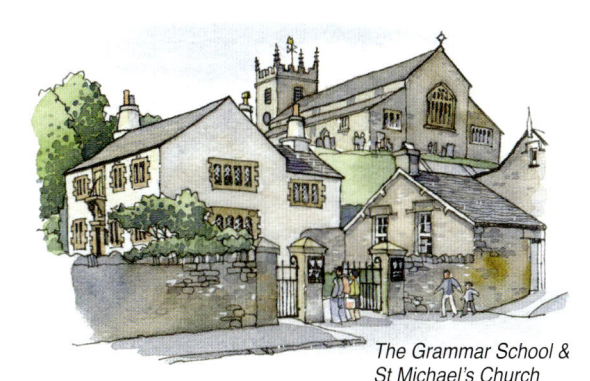

The Grammar School & St Michael's Church

The Minstrel's Gallery & Methodist Chapel

King's Arms Hotel

The Church of St Michael stands on a grassy hill overlooking the village. The present building replaced an ancient chapel in the 15th century.

The schoolboy Wordsworth wrote of its 'snow-white' walls, but they have been unpoetic gray since the rendering was removed in 1875.

ATTRACTION

Beatrix Potter Gallery
Potter sketchbooks, drawings, watercolours, letters and manuscripts, including the original manuscript and illustrations for *The Tale of Peter Rabbit*. Also originals of her delicate botanical illustrations. Hugely popular – you may have to queue.
nationaltrust.org.uk/beatrix-potter-gallery-and-hawkshead

PIT STOPS

Sun Inn
17th-century traditional village inn. Bar meals and restaurant. Serves classic English dishes and locally brewed ales. Rustic-style rooms to let, some with four-posters, beams and exposed stone walls.
suninn.co.uk.

King's Arms
Oak beams and open fires in this 500-year-old inn, which has eight comfortable bedrooms. Real ale and unrivalled range of malt whiskies. Beer garden on the Square.
kingsarmshawkshead.co.uk

Lakeland Icons

8

Lakeland Icons

Leave Hawkshead heading north on the B5285, signed Coniston & Ambleside. About 500yds out of Hawkshead the road turns sharply left signed Hawkshead Hill & Coniston. Climb through rolling hills, patches of woodland and distant fell views to Hawkshead Hill, a picturesque hamlet of white lakeland houses and an ancient baptist chapel dating to 1709. Just beyond the chapel turn right into a narrow road signed Tarn Hows. Join the road from Ambleside for a short distance, then at Summer Hill Country House turn right into a narrow road signed Tarn Hows, a single track road with passing places which twists and climbs through woodland to the famous beauty spot. Continue to the main car park on the western side of the tarns.

Bowfell 2,949ft (902m)
Pike o' Stickle 2,313ft (705m)
Harrison Stickle 2,415ft (736m)
Pavey Ark 2,297ft (700m)
High Raise 2,500ft (762m)
Sergeant Man 2,414ft (736m)
Pike o' Blisco 2,313ft (705m)
Holme Fell 1,040ft (317m)
Rossett Pike 2,136ft (651m)
Loft Crag 2,238ft (682m)
Lingmoor Fell 1,540ft (469m)
Steel Fell 1,814ft (553m)
Low Fell 1,388ft (423m)

Tarn Hows

120

Tarn Hows is not your usual Lakeland tarn. This one has car parks, toilets and over a million visitors a year. The half-mile long tarn, set in a bowl of low and lushly wooded hills, has islands, peninsulas and a panoramic background of fells, surprisingly extensive from such a low vantage point. Like a romantic stage set, the scene is so perfect it looks unreal.

Critics say it is unreal. Tarn Hows is a man-made feature begun around 1914 when the landowners, the Marshall family, built a dam and converted a number of small tarns and marshy ground into one tarn with two little islands. In 1929, when the 4,000-acre Monk Coniston Estate, which included Tarn Hows, was put up for sale, Beatrix Potter bought it. She sold half to the National Trust at cost and bequeathed it the other half.

Extensive landscaping, hard footpaths and footbridges makes it even more artificial every year. Nevertheless, despite its detractors and the sometimes over-crowding, Tarn Hows on a bright, crisp morning is a scene of unforgettable beauty.

8 Lakeland Icons

- Tom Heights 882ft (269m)
- Helvellyn 3,117ft (950m)
- Seat Sandal 2,415ft (736m)
- Dollywaggon Pike 2,815ft (858m)
- Fairfield 2,863ft (874m)
- Hart Crag 2,696ft (822m)
- Dove Crag 2,598ft (792m)
- High Pike 2,150ft (656m)
- Black Fell 1,059ft (323m)
- Red Screes 2,546ft (776m)

8

Return to the Ambleside road along the road you came on. Turn right signed Coniston to rejoin the B5285 at High Cross. Turn right here, twisting downhill through woodland to Coniston lakeside.

As signed, go left for Brantwood, once the home of John Ruskin. The narrow road follows the north eastern side of the lake. Look out for the turning to Bank Ground Tearoom, just beyond Lanehead, a yellow-painted training and activity centre with Ransome connections. Brantwood, with parking, is a mile or so further on.

Brantwood

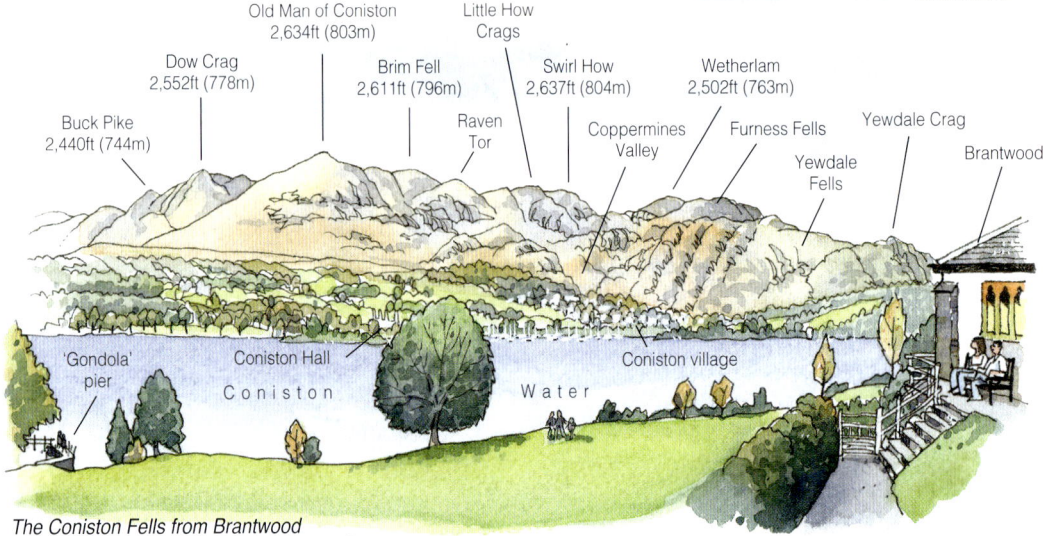

John Ruskin 1819-1900

The leading English art critic of the Victorian era, Ruskin was also an art patron, draughtsman, watercolourist, philosopher, prominent social thinker and philanthropist. His writings emphasised the connections between nature, art and society.

He bought Brantwood in 1871, reputably without seeing the house. It turned out to be little more than a tumbledown 17th-century cottage overlooking Coniston Water, but over the last 30 years of his life Ruskin turned it into a fine country house packed with art treasures. With the estate of over 500 acres, Brantwood is open to the public as he wished.

A florid, carved cross of local slate marks his grave in Coniston churchyard. He also has a monument on Friar's Crag, Derwentwater.

The Coniston Fells from Brantwood

- Buck Pike 2,440ft (744m)
- Dow Crag 2,552ft (778m)
- Old Man of Coniston 2,634ft (803m)
- Brim Fell 2,611ft (796m)
- Raven Tor
- Little How Crags
- Swirl How 2,637ft (804m)
- Coppermines Valley
- Wetherlam 2,502ft (763m)
- Furness Fells
- Yewdale Fells
- Yewdale Crag
- Brantwood
- 'Gondola' pier
- Coniston Hall
- Coniston Water
- Coniston village

Arthur Ransome 1884-1967

Born in Leeds, Ransome bought the first of several houses in the Lakes in 1925. He began to write the first of his 12 *Swallows and Amazons* children's stories in 1929.

Five of them were exclusively set around Coniston Water and Windermere, and reflected his own passions for sailing, camping and fishing.

Donald Campbell (1921-67)

Scarcely a Lakeland icon but Campbell is forever associated with Coniston Water, where he died trying to break his own world waterspeed record of 276mph. His body was retrieved in 2001 and buried in St Andrew's churchyard.

Coniston Water

The lake is just over five miles long, barely half a mile wide and has a maximum depth of around 180ft. Seen from the busy A593 road, Coniston Water can be disappointing. But from the narrow road along the eastern side, the lake is seen at its best with the Old Man of Coniston and its neighbouring fells forming a dramatic background.

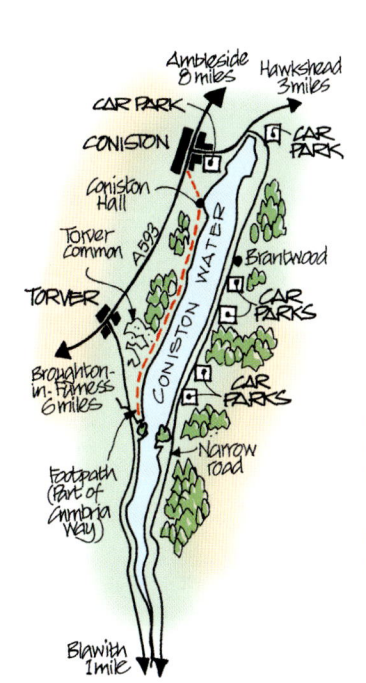

The lake has been a busy waterway for centuries. When mining began in the Coniston Fells ore was shipped for smelting in lakeside bloomeries and south to the lake foot for transportation to Greenodd on the River Leven estuary.

In 1859 the mines were linked to the main coastal railway by a branch line to Broughton on Furness.

But the boom didn't last. By 1890 mining in the area had virtually ceased and the railway closed in 1957.

ATTRACTION

Brantwood

It's said you could spend a day at Brantwood and never be bored. The house has been kept very much as a home and you can enjoy Ruskin's rooms, paintings and fantastic views across the lake. Or just wander around the gardens in the 250-acre estate. There's also a bookshop and an excellent café. *brantwood.org.uk*

PIT STOP

Bank Ground Farm Tearoom

Part of a farm offering self-catering holidays, B&B and Ransome connections, this gem of a tearoom is located on the lakeside with fabulous views and food to match. *bankground.com*

Bank Ground Farm

Lakeland Icons

8 Coniston

Although off the main tourist track through Lakeland, Coniston still attracts its fair share of visitors. An old mining village of grey slate buildings and Victorian shopfronts, it's dominated by rugged fells and retains a utilitarian, rough and ready appeal. The copper mines, for which the area is famous, probably date from Norman times, but were most prosperous during the 16th century when German miners worked here. Tourism is now Coniston's main industry. The village isn't noted for its shopping, but has all the facilities a visitor needs.

Lakeland Icons

Yewdale Road and the Yewdale Fells

Coniston Hall, which dates to around 1250

Church Beck flows through – and occasionally floods – the village from its source high in the hills, still known as Coppermines Valley.

Church Beck and the Coniston Fells

Built in 1856, the steam yacht Gondola sailed on Coniston until decommissioned in 1936. After running aground during a storm in the 1960s, she was left to rot at the lakeside. Eventually, the National Trust restored the vessel and brought her back into service in 1980.

Originally coal-burning, Gondola is now more green and since 2008 has been fired on compressed sawdust logs. She carries up to 86 passengers in considerable luxury with stop-offs at Brantwood

Two ecofriendly Coniston launches, inevitably named *Ruskin* and *Ransome*, are solar-powered wooden vessels providing regular services around the lake. They also sail two specialist routes, one associated with Donald Campbell, the other around southern parts of the lake used as settings for Ransome's *Swallows and Amazons* books, and where the 1974 and 2016 films were shot. Both routes call at Brantwood.

Gondola

ATTRACTION

Ruskin Museum
A mixed bag of Ruskin artifacts including letters, manuscripts, sketchbooks and a pair of his socks! Some of his fine watercolours too. The museum also traces the history of the village and Lakeland life in general.
ruskinmuseum.com

PITSTOPS

Black Bull Inn
Hugely popular village centre pub, noted for its hearty bar meals and Bluebird bitter, an award-winning ale brewed on the premises. Various rooms for B&B stays.
blackbullconiston.co.uk.

Bluebird Café
Terrific location on the lakeside with a covered outdoor terrace. Enjoy Cumberland sausage butties, soups and sandwiches, jacket potatoes and salads. Perfect for a leisurely coffee and cake.
thebluebirdcafe.co.uk

125

8

Lakeland Icons

Leave the village heading north on the A593, a lovely road through typical 'Beatrix Potter' country, twisting and turning, up and down, past woodland crags and sheep. Lookout for High Yewdale Farm, a mile or so out of the village which Potter bought in 1929 as part of the Monk Coniston Estate. The much photographed Yew Tree farm, which the route passes around 60 yards further on, was also part of the estate.

After five lovely miles the road descends to the bridge over the River Brathay, an excellent place to stop, have a look round and perhaps sample the delights at Chesters. (See Tour 4, P59).

Beyond Skelwith Bridge, the A593 swings right to Ambleside, two and a half miles away. Wordsworth had a office in Ambleside when he was Collector of Stamps for the county of Westmorland. (See Tour 4, P61).

Continue on the A591 to the hamlet of Rydal where Wordsworth spent the last 37 years of his life in splendid rural contentment.

Further along the route passes tranquil Rydal Water and Grasmere lake before arriving at Grasmere village, the end of this tour and a mecca for devotees of possibly Lakeland's greatest icon, William Wordsworth.

Yew Tree Farm, which appeared in the 2006 film Miss Potter as Beatrix Potter's home

Rydal Water from the old coffin route behind Rydal Mount

Rydal Water isn't very big, less than a mile long and some 500 yards wide. Almost surrounded by fells and with only one building in sight, Nab Cottage, the lake has a look of remoteness contrary to its actual location, less than a mile from busy Ambleside.

Nab Cottage was once the home of Thomas De Quincey, writer and acquaintance of the Lake Poet's circle.

William Wordsworth (1770-1850)

A true Lakelander, Wordsworth was born in Cockermouth. His parents died early and he was educated at Hawkshead and Cambridge University. He went on walking tours of Europe, visited Paris during the French Revolution and even fathered an illegitimate daughter.

Back in England he went to live in Somerset with his sister Dorothy, where he met Samuel Taylor Coleridge. Together they produced *Lyrical Ballads*, now described as 'one of the turning points in the history of English poetry'.

In 1799 the Wordsworth's returned to the Lakes to live in Grasmere, William's 'Vale of Dreams'. Coleridge followed in 1800, living at Greta Hall in Keswick, where Robert Southy joined him to complete the trio of 'Lake Poets'.

William married Mary Hutchinson in 1802 and they lived, with his sister, in Dove Cottage. By this time Coleridge had become addicted to opium and Wordsworth abandoned him in 1810. They never met again. (See 'The Wordsworth Houses' Tour 3, P39)

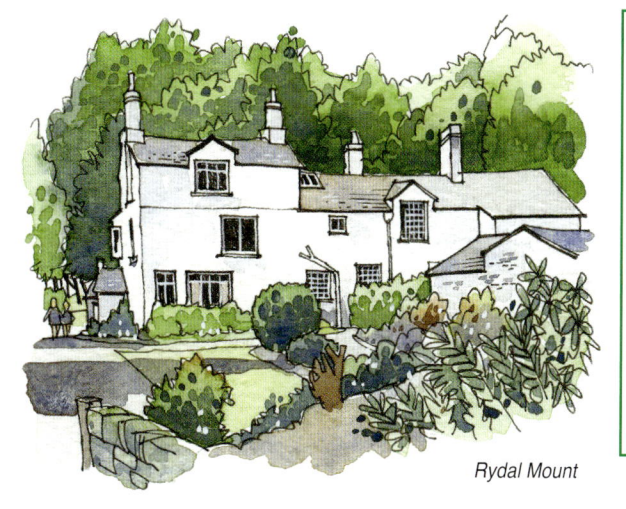

Rydal Mount

Wordsworth never owned his own home but managed to live rather grandly at Rydal Mount for the last 37 years of his life, renting it from the Flemings of nearby Rydal Hall. Dances and dinners were held and prominent people of the day climbed the steep access road to visit. Descendants of the poet subsequently bought Rydal Mount and it has been open to the public since 1970.

William helped to establish – and design – St Mary's church at Rydal, opened in 1824 with Wordsworth a church warden for a year in the 1830s. He bought the field next to the church for his daughter. Bright with a host of dancing daffodils in spring, it's still known as Dora's Field. Following her death in 1847, Wordsworth never wrote another line of poetry.

ATTRACTION
Rydal Mount
A treasure chest of Wordsworth memorabilia in what is still essentially a family home. Personal items abound, from the poet's leather sofa to sister Dorothy's brooch. Wordsworth designed and planted part of the large garden, a cavalcade of lawns, rock pools and shrubs.

There's a tearoom, shop and great views, but minimal parking.
rydalmount.co.uk

St Mary's Church

Also by Jim Watson ...

London's Architectural Walks
A unique guide to the most celebrated landmark buildings in one of the world's major cities. The walks also visit London's most beautiful parks as well as palaces, theatres, museums and some surprising oddities. Enriched with the author's line and watercolour illustrations, this book is the essential companion for anyone interested in the architecture that has shaped this great city.

Touring the Cotswolds
The authoritive guide to exploring the best of the Cotswolds by car. It will guide you to attractions along the way and suggests many award-winning gastropubs and restaurants for which the region is famous. You'll be guided through a maze of country lanes, climb high hills with panoramic views, negotiate woodland, and cross picturesque valleys, providing the most comprehensive portrait of this varied and delightful area.

The Sketchbook Series
Packed with emotive line and watercolour illustrations, maps, facts and figures, history and quirky surprises, these unique books are the perfect guidebook, gift or souvenir.

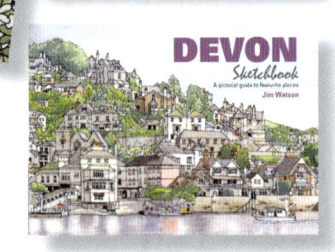

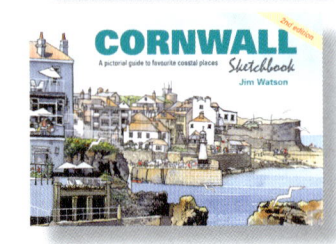

CITY BOOKS
citybooks.co
survivalbooks.net